3rd Workshop on e-Commerce and NLP 2020 (ECNLP 3)

Online
10 July 2020

ISBN: 978-1-7138-1384-2

ECNLP 3

The Workshop on e-Commerce and NLP

Proceedings of the Third Workshop

July 10, 2020

Introduction

It is our great pleasure to welcome you to the Third International Workshop on e-Commerce and NLP (ECNLP).

This workshop focuses on intersection of Natural Language Processing (NLP) and e-Commerce. NLP and information retrieval (IR) have been powering e-Commerce applications since the early days of the fields. Today, NLP and IR already play a significant role in e-Commerce tasks, including product search, recommender systems, product question answering, machine translation, sentiment analysis, product description and review summarization, and customer review processing. With the exploding popularity of chatbots and shopping assistants – both text- and voice-based – NLP, IR, question answering, and dialogue systems research is poised to transform e-Commerce once again.

The ECNLP workshop series was designed to provide a venue for the dissemination of late-breaking research results and ideas related to e-commerce and online shopping, as well as a forum where new and unfinished ideas could be discussed. After the successful ECNLP workshops at The Web Conference in 2019 and 2020, we are happy to host ECNLP 3 at ACL 2020 and once again bring together researchers from both academia and industry.

We have received a larger number of submissions than we could accept for presentation. ECNLP 3 received 21 submissions of long and short research papers. In total, ECNLP 3 featured 13 accepted papers (62% acceptance rate). The selection process was competitive and we believe it resulted in a balanced and varied program that is appealing to audiences from the various sub-areas of e-Commerce.

We would like to thank everyone who submitted a paper to the workshop. We would also like to express our gratitude to the members of the Program Committee for their timely reviews, and for supporting the tight schedule by providing reviews at short notice.

We hope that you enjoy the workshop!

The ECNLP Organizers   May 2020

Organizers:

Shervin Malmasi (Amazon, USA)
Surya Kallumadi (The Home Depot, USA)
Nicola Ueffing (eBay Inc, Germany)
Oleg Rokhlenko (Amazon, USA)
Eugene Agichtein (Emory University, USA)
Ido Guy (eBay Inc, Israel)

Program Committee:

Amita Misra (IBM)
Arushi Prakash (Zulily)
Besnik Fetahu (L3S Research Center / Leibniz University of Hannover)
Cheng Wang (NEC Laboratories Europe)
David Martins de Matos (INESC-ID, Instituto Superior Técnico, Universidade de Lisboa)
Debanjan Mahata (Bloomberg)
Emerson Paraiso (Pontificia Universidade Catolica do Parana)
Giuseppe Castellucci (Amazon)
Gregor Leusch (eBay)
Irina Temnikova (Sofia University, Bulgaria)
Jacopo Tagliabue (Coveo)
Lesly Miculicich (École polytechnique fédérale de Lausanne - Idiap)
Mladen Karan (TakeLab, University of Zagreb)
Raksha Sharma (IIT Roorkee)
Simone Filice (Amazon)
Wai Lam (The Chinese University of Hong Kong)
Xiaoting Zhao (Etsy)
Yitong Li (The University of Melbourne)

Table of Contents

Bootstrapping Named Entity Recognition in E-Commerce with Positive Unlabeled Learning
Hanchu Zhang, Leonhard Hennig, Christoph Alt, Changjian Hu, Yao Meng and Chao Wang.....1

How to Grow a (Product) Tree: Personalized Category Suggestions for eCommerce Type-Ahead
Jacopo Tagliabue, Bingqing Yu and Marie Beaulieu...7

Deep Learning-based Online Alternative Product Recommendations at Scale
Mingming Guo, Nian Yan, Xiquan Cui, San He Wu, Unaiza Ahsan, Rebecca West and Khalifeh Al Jadda...19

A Deep Learning System for Sentiment Analysis of Service Calls
Yanan Jia...24

Using Large Pretrained Language Models for Answering User Queries from Product Specifications
Kalyani Roy, Smit Shah, Nithish Pai, Jaidam Ramtej, Prajit Nadkarni, Jyotirmoy Banerjee, Pawan Goyal and Surender Kumar..35

Improving Intent Classification in an E-commerce Voice Assistant by Using Inter-Utterance Context
Arpit Sharma..40

Semi-Supervised Iterative Approach for Domain-Specific Complaint Detection in Social Media
Akash Gautam, Debanjan Mahata, Rakesh Gosangi and Rajiv Ratn Shah.....................46

Item-based Collaborative Filtering with BERT
Tian Wang and Yuyangzi Fu...54

Semi-supervised Category-specific Review Tagging on Indonesian E-Commerce Product Reviews
Meng Sun, Marie Stephen Leo, Eram Munawwar, Paul C. Condylis, Sheng-yi Kong, Seong Per Lee, Albert Hidayat and Muhamad Danang Kerianto...59

Deep Hierarchical Classification for Category Prediction in E-commerce System
Dehong Gao...64

SimsterQ: A Similarity based Clustering Approach to Opinion Question Answering
Aishwarya Ashok, Ganapathy Natarajan, Ramez Elmasri and Laurel Smith-Stvan.............69

e-Commerce and Sentiment Analysis: Predicting Outcomes of Class Action Lawsuits
Stacey Taylor and Vlado Keselj..77

On Application of Bayesian Parametric and Non-parametric Methods for User Cohorting in Product Search
Shashank Gupta...86

Bootstrapping Named Entity Recognition in E-Commerce with Positive Unlabeled Learning

Hanchu Zhang[1]   Leonhard Hennig[2]   Christoph Alt[2]   Changjian Hu[1]
Yao Meng[1]   Chao Wang[1]

[1]Lenovo Research Artificial Intelligence Lab
[2]German Research Center for Artificial Intelligence (DFKI)
{zhanghc9,hucj1,mengyao1,wangchao31}@lenovo.com
{leonhard.hennig,christoph.alt}@dfki.de

Abstract

Named Entity Recognition (NER) in domains like e-commerce is an understudied problem due to the lack of annotated datasets. Recognizing novel entity types in this domain, such as products, components, and attributes, is challenging because of their linguistic complexity and the low coverage of existing knowledge resources. To address this problem, we present a bootstrapped positive-unlabeled learning algorithm that integrates domain-specific linguistic features to quickly and efficiently expand the seed dictionary. The model achieves an average F1 score of 72.02% on a novel dataset of product descriptions, an improvement of 3.63% over a baseline BiLSTM classifier, and in particular exhibits better recall (4.96% on average).

1 Introduction

The vast majority of existing named entity recognition (NER) methods focus on a small set of prominent entity types, such as persons, organizations, diseases, and genes, for which labeled datasets are readily available (Tjong Kim Sang and De Meulder, 2003; Smith et al., 2008; Weischedel et al., 2011; Li et al., 2016). There is a marked lack of studies in many other domains, such as e-commerce, and for novel entity types, e.g. products and components.

The lack of annotated datasets in the e-commerce domain makes it hard to apply supervised NER methods. An alternative approach is to use dictionaries (Nadeau et al., 2006; Yang et al., 2018), but freely available knowledge resources, e.g. Wikidata (Vrandečic and Krötzsch, 2014) or YAGO (Suchanek et al., 2007), contain only very limited information about e-commerce entities. Manually creating a dictionary of sufficient quality and coverage would be prohibitively expensive. This is amplified by the fact that in the e-commerce domain, entities are frequently expressed as complex noun phrases instead of proper names. Product and component category terms are often combined with brand names, model numbers, and attributes (*"hard drive"* → *"SSD hard drive"* → *"WD Blue 500 GB SSD hard drive"*), which are almost impossible to enumerate exhaustively. In such a low-coverage setting, employing a simple dictionary-based approach would result in very low recall, and yield very noisy labels when used as a source of labels for a supervised machine learning algorithm. To address the drawbacks of dictionary-based labeling, Peng et al. (2019) propose a positive-unlabeled (PU) NER approach that labels positive instances using a seed dictionary, but makes no label assumptions for the remaining tokens (Bekker and Davis, 2018). The authors validate their approach on the CoNLL, MUC and Twitter datasets for standard entity types, but it is unclear how their approach transfers to the e-commerce domain and its entity types.

Contributions We adopt the PU algorithm of Peng et al. (2019) to the domain of consumer electronic product descriptions, and evaluate its effectiveness on four entity types: *Product, Component, Brand* and *Attribute*. Our algorithm bootstraps NER with a seed dictionary, iteratively labels more data and expands the dictionary, while accounting for accumulated errors from model predictions. During labeling, we utilize dependency parsing to efficiently expand dictionary matches in text. Our experiments on a novel dataset of product descriptions show that this labeling mechanism, combined with a PU learning strategy, consistently improves F1 scores over a standard BiLSTM classifier. Iterative learning quickly expands the dictionary, and further improves model performance. The proposed approach exhibits much better recall than the baseline model, and generalizes better to unseen entities.

Proceedings of the 3rd Workshop on e-Commerce and NLP (ECNLP 3), pages 1–6
Online, July 10, 2020. ©2020 Association for Computational Linguistics

Algorithm 1: Iterative Bootstrapping NER

Input: Dictionary D_{seed}, Corpus C,
threshold K, max_iterations I
Result: Dictionary D^+, Classifier L
$D^+ \leftarrow D_{seed}$;
$C_{dep} \leftarrow dependency\_parse(C)$;
$i \leftarrow 0$;
while *not_converged(D^+) and $i < I$* **do**
  $C_{lab} \leftarrow label(C, D^+)$;
  $C_{exp} \leftarrow expand\_labels(C_{lab}, C_{dep})$;
  $L \leftarrow train\_classifier(C_{exp})$;
  $C_{pred} \leftarrow predict(C_{exp}, L)$;
  for $e \leftarrow C_{pred}$ **do**
    if $e \notin D^+$ *and freq(e) > K* **then**
      $D^+ \leftarrow add\_entity(D^+, e)$;
    end
  end
  $i \leftarrow i + 1$;
end

2 NER with Positive Unlabeled Learning

In this section, we first describe the iterative bootstrapping process, followed by our approach to positive unlabeled learning for NER (PU-NER).

2.1 Iterative Bootstrapping

The goal of iterative bootstrapping is to successively expand a seed dictionary of entities to label an existing training dataset, improving the quality and coverage of labels in each iteration (see Algorithm 1). In the first step, we use the seed dictionary to assign initial labels to each token. We then utilize the dependency parses of sentences to label tokens in a "compound" relation with already labeled tokens (see Figure 1). In the example "hard drive" is labeled a *Component* based on the initial seed dictionary, and according to its dependency parse it has a "compound" relation with "dock", which is therefore also labeled as a *Component*. We employ an IO label scheme, because dictionary entries are often more generic than the specific matches in text (see the previous example), which would lead to erroneous tags with schemes such as BIO.

In the second step, we train a NER model on the training dataset with new labels assigned. We repeat these steps at most I times, and in each subsequent iteration we use the trained model to predict new token-level labels on the training data. Novel entities predicted more than K times are included in the dictionary for the next labeling step. The

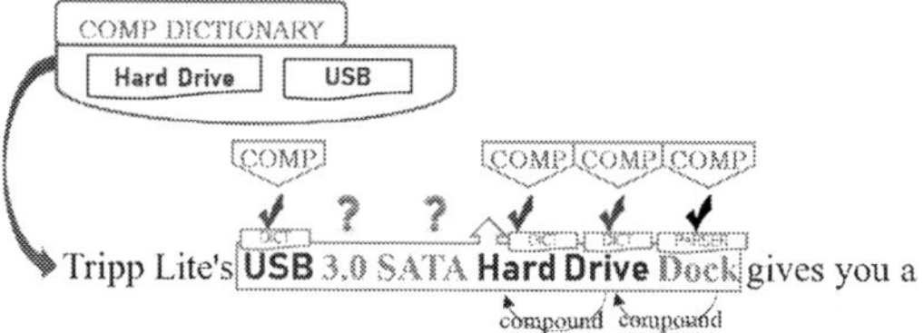

Figure 1: Red check marks indicate tokens labeled by the dictionary, black those based on label expansion using dependency information. The green box shows the true extent of the multi-token *Component* entity.

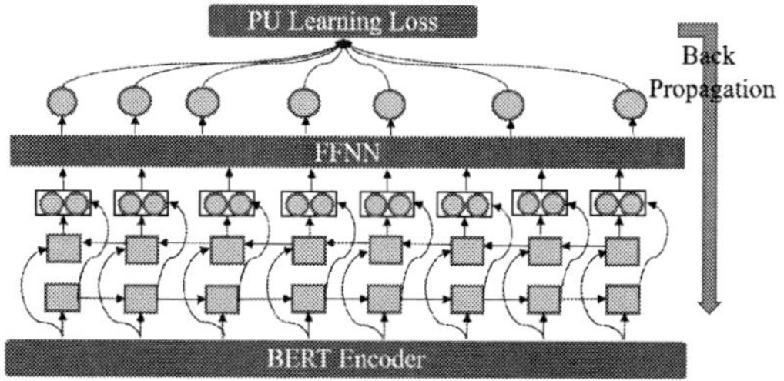

Figure 2: Architecture of the positive unlabeled NER (PU-NER) model.

threshold K ensures that we do not introduce noise in the dictionary with spurious positively labeled entities.

2.2 PU-NER Model

As shown in Figure 2, our model first uses BERT (Devlin et al., 2018) to encode the sub-word tokenized input text into a sequence of contextualized token representations $\{z_1, ..., z_L\}$, followed by a bidirectional LSTM (Lample et al., 2016) layer to model further interactions between tokens. Similar to Devlin et al. (2018), we treat NER as a token-level classification task, without using a CRF to model dependencies between entity labels. We use the vector associated with the first sub-word token in each word as the input to the entity classifier, which consists of a feedforward neural network with a single projection layer. We use back propagation to update the training parameters of the Bi-LSTM and the final classifier, without fine-tuning the entire BERT model.

Dictionary-based labeling achieves high precision on the matched entities but low recall. This fits the positive unlabeled setting (Elkan and Noto, 2008), which assumes that a learner only has access to positive examples and unlabeled data. Thus, we consider all tokens matched by the dictionary as positive, and consider all other tokens to be unlabeled. The goal of PU learning is then to estimate the true risk regarding the expected number of positive examples remaining in the unlabeled data. We define the empirical risk as $\hat{R}_l = \frac{1}{n} \sum_i^n l(\hat{y}_i, y_i)$ and assume the class prior to be equal to real distribution of examples in the data $\pi_p = P(Y = 1)$, and $\pi_n = P(Y = 0)$. As the model tends to predict the positive labels correctly during training, i.e. $l(\hat{y}_i^p, 1)$ declines to a small value. We follow Peng et al. (2019) and combine risk estimation with a non-negative constraint:

$$\hat{R}_l = \frac{1}{n_p} \sum_i^{n_p} l(\hat{y}_i^p, 1)$$
$$+ max\left(0, \frac{1}{n_u} \sum_i^{n_u} l(\hat{y}_i^u, 0) - \frac{\pi_p}{n_p} \sum_i^{n_p} l(\hat{y}_i^p, 0)\right)$$

3 Dataset

E-commerce covers a wide range of complex entity types. In this work, we focus on electronic products, e.g. personal computers, mobile phones, and related hardware, and define the following entity types: **Products**, i.e. electronic consumer devices such as mobiles, laptops, and PCs. *Products* may be preceded by a brand and include some form of model, year, or version specification, e.g. "Galaxy S8" or "Dell Latitude 6400 multimedia notebook". **Components** are parts of a product, typically with a physical aspect, e.g. "battery", or "multimedia keyboard".[1] **Brand** refers to producers of a *product* or *component*, e.g. "Samsung", or "Dell". **Attributes** are units associated with components, e.g. size ("4 TB"), or weight ("3 kg").

To create our evaluation dataset, we use the *Amazon review dataset* (McAuley et al., 2015),[2] a collection of product metadata and customer reviews from Amazon. The metadata includes product title, a descriptive text, category information, price, brand, and image features. We use only entries in the *Electronics/Computers* subcategory and randomly sample product descriptions of length 500–1000 characters, yielding a dataset of 24,272 training documents. We randomly select another 100 product descriptions to form the final test set. These are manually annotated by 2 trained linguists, with disagreements resolved by a third expert annotator. Token-level inter-annotator agreement was

high (Krippendorf's $\alpha = 0.7742$). The test documents contain a total of $27,108$ tokens ($1,493$ *Product*, $3,234$ *Component*, $1,485$ *Attribute*, and 443 *Brand*).

4 Experiments

To evaluate our proposed model (*PU*), we compare it against two baselines: (1) dictionary-only labeling (*Dictionary*), and (2) our model with standard cross-entropy loss instead of the PU learning risk (*BiLSTM*). The *BiLSTM* model is trained in a supervised fashion, treating all non-dictionary entries as negative tokens. The *BiLSTM* and *PU* models were implemented using AllenNLP (Gardner et al., 2018). We use SpaCy[3] for preprocessing, dependency parsing, and dictionary-based entity labeling. We manually define seed dictionaries for *Product* (6 entries), *Component* (60 entries) and *Brand* (13 entries). For *Attributes*, we define a set of 8 regular expressions to pre-label the dataset. Following previous works, we evaluate model performance using token-level F1 score.

There are two options to estimate the value of the class prior π_p. One approach is to treat π_p as a hyperparameter which is fixed during training. Another option is suggested in Peng et al. (2019), who specify an initial value for π_p to start bootstrapping, but recalculate π_p after several train-relabel steps based on the predicted entity type distribution. In our work, we treated π_p as a fixed hyperparameter with a value of $\pi_p = 0.01$.

We run our bootstrapping approach for $I = 10$ iterations, and report the F1 score of the best iteration.

4.1 Results and Discussion

Table 1 shows the F1 scores of several model ablations by entity type on our test dataset. From the table, we can observe: 1) The PU algorithm outperforms the simpler models for most classes, which demonstrates the effectiveness of the PU learning framework for NER in our domain. 2) Dependency parsing is a very effective feature for *Component* and *Product*, and it strongly improves the overall F1 score. 3) The iterative training strategy yields a significant improvement for most classes. Even after several iterations, it still finds new entries to expand the dictionaries (Figure 3).

The *Dictionary* approach shows poor performance on average, which is due to the low recall

---

[1] Non-physical product features and software, such as "Toshiba Face Recognition Software", or "Windows 7" are not considered as components.

[2] http://jmcauley.ucsd.edu/data/amazon/links.html

[3] https://spacy.io/

Entity Type	Dictionary	BiLSTM	PU	PU+Dep	PU+Iter	PU+Dep+Iter
Component	46.19	65.98	66.89	67.38	68.67	**70.66**
Product	16.78	60.23	60.24	65.05	60.24	**67.07**
Brand	49.74	74.06	74.84	**76.24**	**76.24**	76.24
Attribute	7.05	73.30	73.84	**74.14**	**74.14**	**74.14**
All	29.94	68.39	68.95	70.70	69.82	**72.02**

Table 1: Token-Level F1 scores on the test set. The unmodified PU algorithm achieves an average F1 score of 68.95%. Integrating dependency parsing (Dep) and iterative relabeling (Iter) raises the F1 score to 72.02%, an improvement of 42.08% over a dictionary-only approach, and 3.63% over a BiLSTM baseline.

caused by very limited entities in the dictionary. *PU* greatly outperforms the dictionary approach, and has an edge in F1 score over the *BiLSTM* model. The advantages of PU gradually accumulate with each iteration. For *Product*, the combination of PU learning, dependency parsing-based labeling, and iterative bootstrapping, yields a 7% improvement in F1 score, for *Component*, it is still 5%.

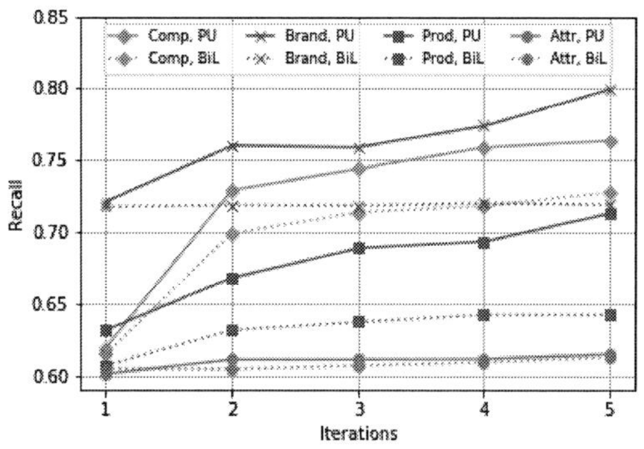

Figure 3: Recall curves of the BiLSTM+Dep and PU+Dep model for *Component*, *Product*, *Brand*, and *Attribute*. PU+Dep boosts recall by 3.03% on average, with a max average difference of 4.96% after 5 iterations.

PU Learning Performance   Figure 3 shows that the *PU* algorithm especially improves recall over the baseline classifier for *Components*, *Products* and *Brands*. With each iteration step, the PU model is increasingly better able to predict unseen entities, and achieves higher recall scores than the BiLSTM model. While the baseline curve on *Brands* stays almost flat during iterations, *PU* consistently improves recall as new entities are added into dictionary. For *Attributes*, however, both models exhibit about the same level of recall, which in addition is largely unaffected by the number of iterations.

This suggests that PU learning better estimates the true loss in the model. In a fully supervised setting, a standard classification loss function can accurately describe the loss on positive and negative samples. However, in the positive unlabeled setting, many unlabeled samples may actually be positive, and therefore the computed loss should not strongly push the model towards the negative class. We therefore want to quantify how much the loss is overestimated due to false negative samples, so that we can appropriately reduce this loss using the estimated real class distribution.

Error Analysis   Both PU and the baseline model in some cases have difficulties predicting *Attributes* correctly. This can be due to spelling differences between train and test data (e.g. "8 Mhz" vs "8Mhz"), but also because of unclean texts in the source documents. Another source of errors is the fixed word piece vocabulary of the pre-trained BERT model, which often splits unit terms such as "Mhz" into several word pieces. Since we use only the first word piece of a token for prediction, this means that signals important for prediction of the *Attribute* class may get lost. This suggests that for technical domains with very specific vocabulary, tokenization is important to allow the model to better represent the meaning of each word piece.

5   Related work

Recent work in positive-unlabeled learning in the area of NLP includes deceptive review detection (Ren et al., 2014), keyphrase extraction (Sterckx et al., 2016) and fact check-worthiness detection (Wright and Augenstein, 2020), see also (Bekker and Davis, 2018) for a survey. Our approach extends the work of Peng et al. (2019) in a novel domain and for challenging entity types. In the area of NER for e-commerce, Putthividhya and Hu (2011) present an approach to extract product attributes and values from product listing titles. Zheng et al. (2018) formulate missing attribute value extraction as a sequence tagging problem, and present a BiLSTM-CRF model with attention. Pazhouhi (2018) studies the problem of product name recognition, but uses a fully supervised approach. In contrast, our method is semi-supervised and uses only very few seed labels.

6 Conclusion

In this work, we introduce a bootstrapped, iterative NER model that integrates a PU learning algorithm for recognizing named entities in a low-resource setting. Our approach combines dictionary-based labeling with syntactically-informed label expansion to efficiently enrich the seed dictionaries. Experimental results on a dataset of manually annotated e-commerce product descriptions demonstrate the effectiveness of the proposed framework.

Acknowledgments

We would like to thank the reviewers for their valuable comments and feedback. Christoph Alt and Leonhard Hennig have been partially supported by the German Federal Ministry for Economic Affairs and Energy as part of the project PLASS (01MD19003E).

References

Jessa Bekker and Jesse Davis. 2018. Learning from positive and unlabeled data: A survey. *CoRR*, abs/1811.04820.

Jacob Devlin, Ming-Wei Chang, Kenton Lee, and Kristina Toutanova. 2018. BERT: pre-training of deep bidirectional transformers for language understanding. *CoRR*, abs/1810.04805.

Charles Elkan and Keith Noto. 2008. Learning classifiers from only positive and unlabeled data. In *Proceedings of the 14th ACM SIGKDD international conference on Knowledge discovery and data mining*, pages 213–220.

Matt Gardner, Joel Grus, Mark Neumann, Oyvind Tafjord, Pradeep Dasigi, Nelson F. Liu, Matthew Peters, Michael Schmitz, and Luke Zettlemoyer. 2018. AllenNLP: A deep semantic natural language processing platform. In *Proceedings of Workshop for NLP Open Source Software (NLP-OSS)*, pages 1–6, Melbourne, Australia. Association for Computational Linguistics.

Guillaume Lample, Miguel Ballesteros, Sandeep Subramanian, Kazuya Kawakami, and Chris Dyer. 2016. Neural architectures for named entity recognition. In *Proceedings of the 2016 Conference of the North American Chapter of the Association for Computational Linguistics: Human Language Technologies*, pages 260–270, San Diego, California. Association for Computational Linguistics.

Jiao Li, Yueping Sun, Robin J. Johnson, Daniela Sciaky, Chih-Hsuan Wei, Robert Leaman, Allan Peter Davis, Carolyn J. Mattingly, Thomas C. Wiegers, and Zhiyong Lu. 2016. Biocreative v cdr task corpus: a resource for chemical disease relation extraction. *Database : the journal of biological databases and curation*, 2016.

Julian J. McAuley, Christopher Targett, Qinfeng Shi, and Anton van den Hengel. 2015. Image-based recommendations on styles and substitutes. *Proceedings of the 38th International ACM SIGIR Conference on Research and Development in Information Retrieval*.

David Nadeau, Peter D. Turney, and Stan Matwin. 2006. Unsupervised named-entity recognition: Generating gazetteers and resolving ambiguity. In *Advances in Artificial Intelligence*, pages 266–277, Berlin, Heidelberg. Springer Berlin Heidelberg.

Elnaz Pazhouhi. 2018. Automatic product name recognition from short product descriptions. Master's thesis, University of Twente.

Minlong Peng, Xiaoyu Xing, Qi Zhang, Jinlan Fu, and Xuanjing Huang. 2019. Distantly supervised named entity recognition using positive-unlabeled learning. In *Proceedings of the 57th Annual Meeting of the Association for Computational Linguistics*, pages 2409–2419, Florence, Italy. Association for Computational Linguistics.

Duangmanee Putthividhya and Junling Hu. 2011. Bootstrapped named entity recognition for product attribute extraction. In *Proceedings of the 2011 Conference on Empirical Methods in Natural Language Processing*, pages 1557–1567, Edinburgh, Scotland, UK. Association for Computational Linguistics.

Yafeng Ren, Donghong Ji, and Hongbin Zhang. 2014. Positive unlabeled learning for deceptive reviews detection. In *Proceedings of the 2014 Conference on Empirical Methods in Natural Language Processing (EMNLP)*, pages 488–498, Doha, Qatar. Association for Computational Linguistics.

Larry Smith, Lorraine K. Tanabe, Rie Johnson nee Ando, Cheng-Ju Kuo, I-Fang Chung, Chun-Nan Hsu, Yu-Shi Lin, Roman Klinger, Christoph M. Friedrich, Kuzman Ganchev, Manabu Torii, Hongfang Liu, Barry Haddow, Craig A. Struble, Richard J. Povinelli, Andreas Vlachos, William A. Baumgartner, Lawrence E. Hunter, Bob Carpenter, Richard Tzong-Han Tsai, Hong-Jie Dai, Feng Liu, Yifei Chen, Chengjie Sun, Sophia Katrenko, Pieter Adriaans, Christian Blaschke, Rafael Torres, Mariana Neves, Preslav Nakov, Anna Divoli, Manuel J. Maña-López, Jacinto Mata, and W. John Wilbur. 2008. Overview of biocreative ii gene mention recognition. *Genome Biology*, 9:S2 – S2.

Lucas Sterckx, Cornelia Caragea, Thomas Demeester, and Chris Develder. 2016. Supervised keyphrase extraction as positive unlabeled learning. In *Proceedings of the 2016 Conference on Empirical Methods in Natural Language Processing*, pages 1924–1929, Austin, Texas. Association for Computational Linguistics.

Fabian M. Suchanek, Gjergji Kasneci, and Gerhard Weikum. 2007. Yago: A core of semantic knowledge. In *Proceedings of the 16th International Conference on World Wide Web*, WWW '07, page 697–706, New York, NY, USA. Association for Computing Machinery.

Erik F. Tjong Kim Sang and Fien De Meulder. 2003. Introduction to the conll-2003 shared task: Language-independent named entity recognition. In *Proceedings of CoNLL-2003*, pages 142–147. Edmonton, Canada.

Denny Vrandečic and Markus Krötzsch. 2014. Wikidata: A free collaborative knowledgebase. *Commun. ACM*, 57(10):78–85.

Ralph Weischedel, Eduard Hovy, Mitchell Marcus, Martha Palmer, Robert Belvin, Sameer Pradhan, Lance Ramshaw, and Nianwen Xue. 2011. *OntoNotes: A Large Training Corpus for Enhanced Processing*.

Dustin Wright and Isabelle Augenstein. 2020. Fact check-worthiness detection as positive unlabelled learning. *ArXiv*, abs/2003.02736.

Yaosheng Yang, Wenliang Chen, Zhenghua Li, Zhengqiu He, and Min Zhang. 2018. Distantly supervised NER with partial annotation learning and reinforcement learning. In *Proceedings of the 27th International Conference on Computational Linguistics*, pages 2159–2169, Santa Fe, New Mexico, USA. Association for Computational Linguistics.

Guineng Zheng, Subhabrata Mukherjee, Xin Dong, and Feifei Li. 2018. Opentag: Open attribute value extraction from product profiles. *Proceedings of the 24th ACM SIGKDD International Conference on Knowledge Discovery & Data Mining*.

How to Grow a (Product) Tree
Personalized Category Suggestions for eCommerce Type-Ahead

Jacopo Tagliabue
Coveo Labs, New York, USA
jtagliabue@coveo.com

Bingqing Yu
Coveo, Montreal, CA
cyu2@coveo.com

Marie Beaulieu
Coveo, Quebec, CA
mabeaulieu@coveo.com

Abstract

In an attempt to balance precision and recall in the search page, leading digital shops have been effectively nudging users into select category facets as early as in the type-ahead suggestions. In *this* work, we present **Session-Path**, a novel neural network model that improves facet suggestions on two counts: first, the model is able to leverage session embeddings to provide scalable personalization; second, **SessionPath** predicts facets by *explicitly* producing a probability distribution at each node in the taxonomy path. We benchmark **SessionPath** on two partnering shops against count-based and neural models, and show how business requirements and model behavior can be combined in a principled way.

1 Introduction

Modern eCommerce search engines need to work on millions of products; in an effort to fight "zero result" pages, digital shops often sacrifice *precision* to increase *recall*[1], relying on *Learn2Rank* (Liu, 2009) to show the most relevant results in the top positions (Matveeva et al., 2006). While this strategy is effective in web search, when users rarely go after page one (Granka et al., 2004; Guan and Cutrell, 2007), it is only partially successful in product search: shoppers may spend time browsing several pages in the result set and *re-order* products based on custom criteria (Figure 1); analyzing industry data, up to 20% of clicked products occur *not* on the first page, with re-ranking in approximately 10% of search sessions.

Leading eCommerce websites leverage machine learning to suggest *facets* - i.e. product categories, such as *Video Games* for "nintendo switch" - *during*

Figure 1: Price re-ordering on *Amazon.com*, showing degrading relevance in the result set when querying for a console - "nintendo switch" - and then re-ranking based on price.

type-ahead (Figure 2): narrowing down candidate products explicitly by matching the selected categories, shops are able to present less noisy result pages and increase the perceived relevance of their search engine. In *this* work we present **Session-Path**, a scalable and personalized model to solve facet prediction for type-ahead suggestions: given a shopping session and candidate queries in the suggestion dropdown menu, the model is asked to predict the best category facet to help users narrow down search intent. A big advantage of **Session-Path** is that it can complement any existing stack by adding facet prediction to items as retrieved by the type-ahead API.

We summarize the main contributions of *this* work as follows:

- we devise, implement and benchmark several models of incremental complexity (as measured by features and engineering requirements); starting from a non-personalized count-based baseline, we arrive at **Session-Path**, an encoder-decoder architecture that explicitly models the real-time generation of paths in the catalog taxonomy;

---

[1]The "nintendo switch" query for a gaming console returns 50k results on *Amazon.com* at the time of drafting this footnote; 50k results are more products than the entire catalog of a mid-size shop such as **Shop 1** below.

Proceedings of the 3rd Workshop on e-Commerce and NLP (ECNLP 3), pages 7–18
Online, July 10, 2020. ©2020 Association for Computational Linguistics

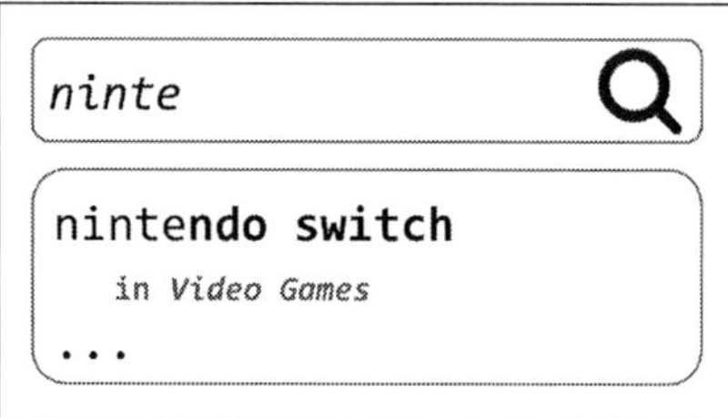

Figure 2: Facet suggestions during type-ahead: shoppers can be nudged to pick a facet *before* querying, to help the search engine present more relevant results.

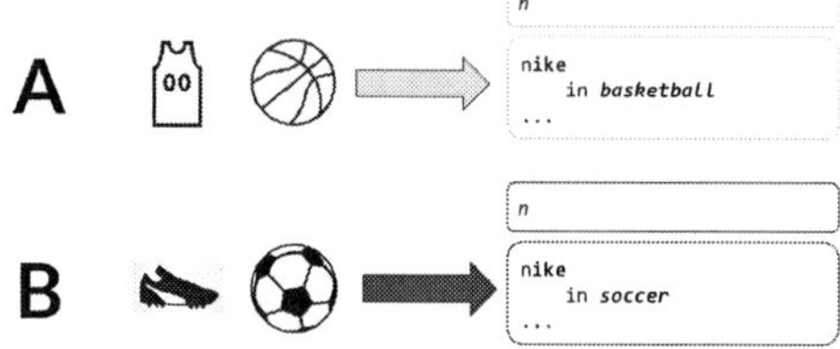

Figure 3: Shoppers in **Session A** and **Session B** have different sport intent, as shown by the products visited. By combining linguistic and behavioral in-session data, **SessionPath** provides in real-time personalized facet suggestions to the same "nike" query in the type-ahead.

- we discuss the importance of false positives and false negatives in the relevant business context, and provide decision criteria to adjust the precision/recall boundary after training. By combining the predictions of the neural network with a *decision module*, we show how model behavior can be tuned in a principled way by human decision makers, without interfering with the underlying inference process or introducing *ad hoc* manual rules.

To the best of our knowledge, **SessionPath** is the first type-ahead model that allows *dynamic* facet predictions: linguistic input and in-session intent are combined to adjust the target taxonomy depth (*sport / basketball* vs *sport / basketball / lebron*) based on real-time shopper behavior and model confidence. For this reason, we believe the methods and results here presented will be of great interest to any digital shop struggling to strike the right balance between precision and recall in a catalog with tens-of-thousands-to-millions of items.

2 Less (Choice) is More: Considerations From Industry Use Cases

The problem of narrowing down the result set before re-ranking is a known concern for mid-to-big-size shops: as shown in Figure 1-A, a common solution is to invite shoppers to select a category facet when still typing. Aside from UX considerations, restricting the result set may be beneficial for other reasons. On one hand, decision science proved that providing shoppers with *more* alternatives is actually less efficient (the so-called "paradox of choice" (Scheibehenne et al., 2010; Iyengar and Lepper, 2001)) - insofar as **SessionPath** helps avoiding unnecessary "cognitive load", it may be a welcomed ally in fighting irrational decision making; on the other, by restricting result set through

facet selection, the model may reduce the long-tail effect of many queries on product visibility: when results are too many and items frequently changed, standard *Learn2Rank* approaches tend to penalize less popular items (Abdollahpouri et al., 2017; Anderson, 2006), which end up buried among noisy results far from the first few pages and never collect enough relevance feedback to rise through the top.

In *this* work, we extend industry best practices of facet suggestion in type-ahead by providing a solution that is dynamic in two ways: i) given the same query, session context may be used to provide a contextualized suggestion (Figure 3); ii) given two queries, the model will decide in real-time how deep in the taxonomy path the proposed suggestion needs to be (Figure 4): for some queries, a generic facet may be optimal (as we do not want to narrow the result set *too much*), for others a more specific suggestion may be more suitable. Given the natural trade-off between *precision* and *recall* at different depths, Section 7.2 is devoted to provide a principled solution.

3 Related Work

Facet selection. Facet selection is linked to *query classification* on the research side (Lin et al., 2018; Skinner and Kallumadi, 2019) and *query scoping* on the product side, i.e. pre-selecting, say, the facet *color* with value *black* for a query such as "black basketball shoes" (Liberman and Lempel, 2014; Vandic et al., 2013). Scoping may result in an aggressive restriction of the result set, lowering *recall* excessively: in most cases, an acceptable shopping experience would need to combine scoping with *query expansion* (Diaz et al., 2016). **SessionPath** is more flexible than query classification, by supporting explicit path prediction and incorporating in-session information; it is more gentle than scop-

8

ing (by nudging transparently the final user instead of forcing a selection behind the scene); it is more principled than expansion in balancing precision and recall.

Deep Learning in IR. The development of deep learning models for IR has been mostly restricted to the retrieve-and-rerank paradigm (Mitra and Craswell, 2017; Guo et al., 2016). Some recent works have been focused specifically on ranking suggestions for type-ahead: neural language models are proposed by Park and Chiba (2017); Wang et al. (2018b); specifically in eCommerce, Kannadasan and Aslanyan (2019) employs *fastText* to represent queries in the ranking phase and Yu et al. (2020) leverages deep image features for in-session personalization. While *this* work employs deep neural networks both for feature encoding and the inference itself, the proposed methods are agnostic on the underlying retrieval algorithm, as long as platforms can enrich type-ahead response with the predicted category. By providing a gentle entry point into existing workflows, a great product strength of **SessionPath** is the possibility of deploying the new functionalities with minimal changes to any architecture, neural or traditional (see also Appendix A).

4   Problem Statement

Suggesting a category facet can be modelled with the help of few formal definitions. A target shop E has products $p_1, p_2, ...p_n \in P$ (e.g. *nike air max 97*) and categories $c_{1,1}, c_{1,2}, ...c_{n,m} \in C$, where $c_{n,m}$ is the category n at *depth* m (e.g. at $m = 1$, [*soccer, volley, football, basketball*], at $m = 2$ [*shoes, pants, t-shirts*], etc.); a taxonomy tree T_m is an *indexed* mapping $P \mapsto C_m$, assigning a category to products for each depth m (e.g. *air max 97* $\mapsto_0$ *root*,$\mapsto_1$ *soccer*, $\mapsto_2$ *shoes*, $\mapsto_3$ *messi* etc.); *root* is the base category in the taxonomy, and it is common to all products (we will omit it for brevity in all our examples). In what follows, we use *path* to denote a sequence of categories (hierarchically structured) in our target shop (e.g. *root / soccer / shoes / messi*), and *nodes* to denote the categories in a path (e.g. *soccer* is a node of *soccer / shoes / messi*).

Given a browsing session s containing products $p_x, p_y, ...p_z$, and a candidate type-ahead query q, the model's goal is to learn both the optimal depth value m and, for each $k \leq m$, a contextual function $f(q, s) \mapsto C_k$. As we shall see in the ensuing

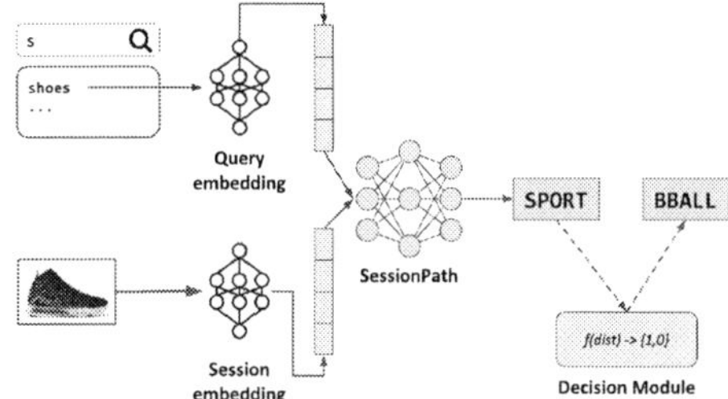

Figure 4: Functional flow for **SessionPath**: the current session and the candidate query "shoes" are embedded and fed to the model; the distribution over possible categories at each step of the taxonomy is passed to a *decision module*, that either cuts the generation at that step or includes the step in the final prediction. The decision process is repeated until either the module cuts or a max-length path is generated.

section, **SessionPath** solution to this challenge is two-fold: a model generating a path first, and a decision module to pick the appropriate depth m (Figure 4).

5   Baseline and Personalized Models

We approach the challenge *incrementally*, by first developing a count-based model (**CM**) that learns a mapping from queries to all paths (i.e. *sport* and *sport / soccer* are treated purely as "labels", so they are two completely unrelated target classes for the model); **CM** will both serve as a baseline for more sophisticated methods and as a fast reference implementation not requiring any deep learning infrastructure. We improve on **CM** with **SessionPath**, a model based on deep neural networks. From a product perspective, it is important to remember (Figure 4) that a *decision module* is called *after* a path prediction is made: we discuss how to tune this crucial part after establishing the general performance of the proposed models.

5.1   A Baseline Model

The intuition behind the count-based model is that we may gain insights on relevant paths linked to a query from the clicks on search results. Therefore, we can build a simple count-based model by creating a map from each query in the search logs to their frequently associated paths. To build this map, we first retrieve all products clicked after each query, along with their path; for a given query, we can then calculate the percentage of occurrence of each path in the clicked products. Since the model is not hierarchical, it is important to note that *sport* and *sport / basketball* will be treated as completely disjoint target classes for the prediction. To avoid noisy results, we empirically determined a frequency threshold for paths to be counted as relevant to a certain query (80%); at prediction time, given a query in the training set, we retrieve all the paths associated with it and return the one with longest depth; for unseen queries, no prediction is made.

5.2 Modelling Session Context and Taxonomy Paths

The main conceptual improvements over **CM** are three:

- **SessionPath** produces predictions also for queries not in the training set;

- **SessionPath** introduces personalization, by combining the linguistic information contained in the query with in-session shopping intent;

- **SessionPath** is trained to produce the most accurate path by explicitly making a new prediction *at each node*, not predicting paths in a *one-out-of-many* scenario; in other words, **SessionPath** knows that *sport* and *sport / basketball* are related, and that the second path is generated from the first when a given distribution over sport activities is present.

To represent the current session in a dense architecture, we first train a skip-gram *prod2vec* model over user data for the entire website, mapping product to 50-dimensional vectors (Mikolov et al., 2013a; Grbovic et al., 2015). At training and serving time **SessionPath** retrieves the embeddings of the products in the target session, and use average pooling to calculate the context vector from the sequence of embeddings, as shown by Covington et al. (2016); Yu et al. (2020). To represent the candidate query, an encoding of linguistic behavior that generalizes to unseen queries is needed. We tested different strategies:

- *word2vec*: we train a skip-gram model from Mikolov et al. (2013b) over product short descriptions from the catalog. Since most search queries are less than three words long, we opted for a simple and fast average pooling of the embeddings in the tokenized query;

- *character-based language model*: inspired by Skinner (2018), we train a char-based language model (single LSTM layer with hidden dimension 50) on search logs and product descriptions from the target shop; a standard LSTM approach was found ineffective in preliminary tests, so we opted instead for using the "Balanced pooling" strategy from Skinner and Kallumadi (2019), where the dense representation for the query is obtained by taking the last network state and then concatenating it together with average-pooling (Wang et al., 2018a), max-pooling, and min-pooling;

- *pre-trained language model*: we map the query to a 768-size vector using BERT (Devlin et al., 2019) (as pre-trained for the target language by Magnini et al. (2006));

- *Search2Prod2Vec + unigrams*: we propose a "small-data" variation to *Search2Vec* by Grbovic et al. (2016), where queries (on a web search engine) are embedded through events happening before and after the search event. Adapting the intuition to product search, we propose to represent queries through the embeddings of products clicked in the search result page; in particular, each query q is the weighted average of the corresponding *prod2vec* embeddings; it can be argued that the *clicking* event is analogous to a "pointing" signal (Tagliabue and Cohn-Gordon, 2019), when the *meaning* of a word ("shoes") is understood as a function from the string to a set of objects falling under that concept (e.g. Chierchia and McConnell-Ginet (2000)). In the spirit of compositional semantics (Baroni et al., 2014), we generalize this representation to unseen queries by building a unigram-based language model, so that "nike shoes" gets its meaning from the composition (average pooling) of the meaning of *nike* and *shoes*.

To generate a path explicitly, we opted for an encoder-decoder architecture. The encoder employs the wide-and-deep approach popularized by Cheng et al. (2016), and concatenates textual and non-textual feature to obtain a wide representation of the current context, which is passed through a dense layer to represent the final encoded state. The decoder is a word-based language model (Zoph and Le, 2016) which produces a sequence of nodes (e.g.

Shop	Queries (with context)	Products
Shop 1	270K (185K)	29.699
Shop 2	270K (227K)	93.967

Table 1: Descriptive statistics for the dataset.

sport, basketball, etc.) conditioned on the representation created by the encoder; more specifically, the architecture of the decoder consists of a single LSTM with 128 cells, a fully-connected layer and a final layer with softmax output activation. The output dimension corresponds to the total number of distinct nodes found in all the paths of the training data, including two additional tokens to encode the start-of-sequence and end-of-sequence. For training, the decoder uses the encoded information to fill its initial cell states; at each timestep, we use teacher forcing to pass the target character, offset by one position, as the next input character to the decoder (Williams and Zipser, 1989). Empirically, we found that robust parameters for the deep learning methods are a learning rate of 0.001, time decay of 0.00001, early stopping with $patience = 20$, and mini-batch of size 128; furthermore, the Adam optimizer with cross-entropy loss is used for all networks, with training up to 300 epochs. Once trained, the model can generate a path given an encoded session representation and a start-of-sequence token: after the first step, the decoder uses autoregression sequence generation (Bahdanau et al., 2015) to predict the next output token.

6 Dataset

We leverage behavioral and search data from two partnering shops in *Company*'s network: **Shop 1** and **Shop 2** have uniform data ingestion, making it easy to compare how well models generalize; they are mid-size shops, with annual revenues between 20 and 100 million dollars. **Shop 1** and **Shop 2** differ however in many respects: they are in different verticals (*apparel* vs *home improvement*), they have a different catalog structure (603 paths organized in 2-to-4 levels for each product vs 985 paths in 3 levels for all products), and different traffic (top 200k vs top 15k in the Alexa Ranking). Descriptive statistics for the training dataset can be found in Table 1: data is sampled for both shops from June-August in 2019; for testing purposes, a completely disjoint dataset is created using events from the month of September.

Model	D=1	D=2	D=last
CM	0.63	0.53	0.22
MLP+BERT	0.72	0.59	0.33
SP+BERT	0.77	0.64	0.40
SP+LSTM	0.79	0.68	0.43
SP+W2V	0.82	0.71	0.46
SP+SV	**0.87**	**0.79(0.01)**	**0.55**
CM	0.41	0.34	0.24
MLP+BERT	0.61	0.50	0.39
SP+BERT	0.66	0.55	0.45
SP+LSTM	0.67	0.57	0.46
SP+W2V	0.69	0.59	0.47
SP+SV	**0.80**	**0.71**	**0.59**

Table 2: Accuracy scores for $depth = 1$, $depth = 2$, $depth = last$, divided by **Shop 1** (*top*) and **Shop 2** (*bottom*). We report the mean over 5 runs, with SD if $SD \geq 0.01$.

7 Experiments

We perform offline experiments using search logs for **Shop 1** and **Shop 2**: for each search event in the dataset, we use products seen before the query (if any) to build a session vector as explained in Section 5.2; the path of the products *clicked after* the query is used as the target variable for the model under examination.

7.1 Making predictions

We benchmark **CM** and **SessionPath** from Section 5, plus a multi-layer perceptron (**MLP**) to investigate the performance of an intermediate model: while not as straightforward as **CM**, **MLP** is considerably easier to train and serve than **Session-Path** and it may therefore be a compelling architectural choice for many shops (see Appendix A for practical engineering details); **MLP** concatenates the session vector with the *BERT* encoding of the candidate query, and produces a distribution over all possible *full-length* paths (*one-out-of-many* classification, where the target class comprises all the paths at the maximum depth for the catalog at hand). Table 2 shows accuracy scores for three different depth levels in the predicted path: **SP+BERT** is **SessionPath** using *BERT* to encode linguistic behavior, **SP+W2V** is using *word2vec*, **SP+SV** is using *Search2Prod2Vec* and **SP+LSTM** is using the language model. Every **SessionPath** variant outperforms the count-based and neural baselines, with *Search2Prod2Vec* providing up to 150% increase over **CM** and 67% over **MLP**. **CM** score is penalized not only by the inability to generalize to unseen queries: even when considering previously seen queries in the test set, **SP+SV**'s accuracy is significantly higher (0.58 vs 0.27 at $D = last$), showing that neural methods are more effective in capturing the underlying dynamics. Linguistic representations learned *directly* over the target shop outperform bigger models pre-trained on generic text sources, highlighting some differences between general-purpose embeddings and shop-specific ones, and suggesting that off-the-shelf NLP models may not be readily applied to short, keyword-based queries. While fairly accurate, **SP+W2V** is much slower to train compared to **SP+SV** and harder to scale across clients, as it relies on having enough content in the catalog to train models that successfully deal with shop lingo. On a final language-related note, it is worth stressing that click-based embeddings built for **SP+SV** show not just better performance over *seen* queries (which is expected), but better generalization ability in the *unseen* part as well compared to *BERT* embeddings (0.82 vs 0.70 at $D = 1$ for **Shop 1**, 0.76 vs 0.63 for **Shop 2**).

In the spirit of ablation studies, we re-run **SP+SV** and **SP+BERT** *without* session vector. Interestingly enough, context seems to play a slightly different role in the two shops and the two models: **SP+BERT** is greatly helped by contextual information, especially for *unseen* queries (0.28 vs 0.21 at $D = last$ for **Shop 1**, 0.40 vs 0.15 for **Shop 2**), but the effect for **SP+SV** is smaller (0.50 vs 0.42 for **Shop 2**); while models on **Shop 2** show a bigger drop in performance when removing session information, generally (and unsurprisingly) session-aware models provide better generalization on *unseen* queries across the board. By comparing **SessionPath** with a simpler neural model (such as **MLP**), it is clear that session plays a bigger role in *MLP*, suggesting that **SessionPath** architecture is able to better leverage linguistic information across cases.

Finally, we investigate sample efficiency of chosen methods by training on smaller fractions of the original training dataset: Table 3 reports accuracy of four methods when downsampling the training set for **Shop 1** to $1/10^{th}$ and $1/4^{th}$ of the dataset size. **CM**'s inability to generalize cripples its total score; **MLP** is confirmed to be simple yet effective, performing significantly better than the count-based baseline; **SP+SV** is confirmed to be

Model (D=last)	1/10	1/4
CM	0.18	0.20
MLP+BERT	0.28	0.30
SP+BERT	0.31	0.34
SP+SV	**0.51**	**0.53**

Table 3: Accuracy scores (**D=last**) when training on portions of the original dataset for **Shop 1**.

the best performing model, and even with only $1/10^{th}$ of samples outperforms all other models from Table 2: by leveraging the bias encoded in the hierarchical structure of the products, **SP+SV** allows paths that share nodes (*sport, sport / basketball*) to also share statistical evidence, resulting in a very efficient learning.

Accuracy provides a strong argument on the efficacy of the proposed models in industry, and it is in fact widely employed in the relevant literature: Vandic et al. (2013) employs click-based accuracy for label prediction, while Molino et al. (2018) (in a customer service use cases) uses accuracy at different depths for sequential predictions that are somewhat similar to **SessionPath**. However, *accuracy* by itself falls short to tell the whole story on product decisions: working with *Coveo*'s clients, it is clear that not all shops are born equal - some (e.g. mono-brand fashion shops) strongly favor a smaller and cleaner result page; others (e.g. marketplaces) favor bigger, even if noisier, result sets. Section 7.2 presents our contribution in analyzing the business context and proposes viable solutions.

7.2 Tuning the decision module

Consider the two possible decisions in the scenario depicted in Figure 5: given "nike shoes" as query and basketball shoes as session context, **SessionPath** prediction is *shoes / nike / basketball*. According to scenario **1**, a decision is made to cut the path at *shoes / nike*: the resulting set of products contain a mixed set of shoes from the target brand, with no specific sport affinity; in scenario **2**, the decision module allows the prediction of a longer path, *shoes / nike / basketball*: the result page is smaller and only contains basketball shoes of the target brand. Intuitively, a perfect model would choose **2** only when it is "confident" of the underlying intention, as expressed through the combination of language and behavioral clues; when the model is less confident, it should stick to **1** to avoid hiding from the shopper's possible interesting products.

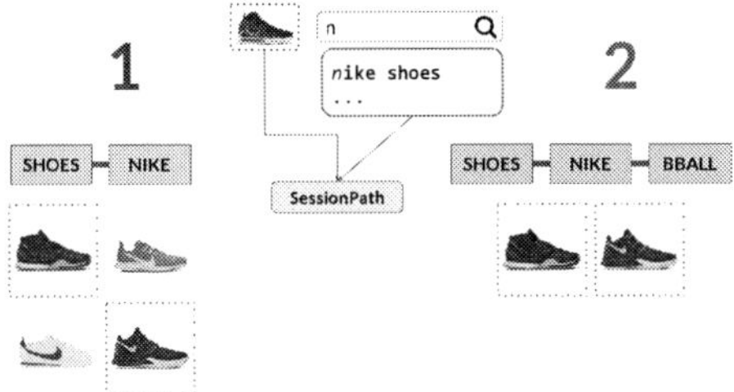

Figure 5: Two scenarios for the decision module after **SessionPath** generates the *shoes / nike / basketball* path, with input query "nike shoes" and Lebron James basketball shoes in the session. In *Scenario 1 (blue)*, we cut the result set after the second node - *shoes / nike* - resulting in a mix set of shoes; in *Scenario 2 (red)*, we use the full path - *shoes / nike / basketball* - resulting in only basketball shoes (dotted line products). How can we define what is the optimal choice?

To quantify how much confident the model is at any given node in the predicted path, at each node s_n we output the multinomial distribution d over the next node s_{n+1}[2] and calculate the Gini coefficient of d, $g(d)$:

$$g(d) = \frac{\sum_{i=1}^{n} \sum_{j=1}^{n} |x_i - x_j|}{2n^2 \bar{x}} \qquad \text{(GI)}$$

where n is the total number of classes in the distribution d, x_i is the probability of the class i and $\bar{x}$ is the mean probability of the distribution.

Once $GI = g(d)$ is computed, a *decision rule* $DR(GI)$ for the decision module in Figure 4 is given by:

$$DR(x) = \begin{cases} 1 & \text{if } x \geq ct \\ 0 & \text{otherwise} \end{cases}$$

where 1 means that the module is confident enough to add the node to the final path that will be shown to the user, while 0 means the path generation is stopped at the current node. ct is our *confidence threshold*: since different values of ct imply more or less aggressive behavior from the model, it is important to tune ct by taking into account the relevant business constraints.

____

[2] Non-existent paths account for less then 0.005% of all the paths in the test set, proving that **SessionPath** is able to accurately learn transitions between nodes and suggesting that an explicit check at decision time is unnecessary. Of course, if needed, a "safety check" may be performed at query time by the search engine, to verify that filtering by the suggested path will result in a non-empty set.

Gini Threshold	Precision	Recall
0.996	0.65	0.99
0.993	0.82	0.91
0.990	0.93	0.77
0.980	0.99	0.74

Table 4: Precision and recall at different decision thresholds for **Shop 1**.

Due to the contextual and interactive nature of **SessionPath**, we turn search logs into a "simulation" of the interactions between hypothetical shoppers and our model (Kuzi et al., 2019). In particular, for any given search event in the test dataset - comprising products seen in the session, the actual query issued, all the products returned by the search engine, the products clicked from the shopper in the result page -, and a model prediction (e.g. *sport / basketball*), we construct two items:

- **golden truth set**: which is the set of the paths corresponding to the items the shopper deemed relevant in that context (relevance is therefore assessed as *pseudo-feedback* from clicks);

- **filtered result set**: which is the set of products returned by the engine, *filtering* out those not matching the prediction by the model (i.e. simulating the engine is actually working with the categories suggested by **SessionPath**).

With the *golden truth set*, the *filtered result set* and the original *result page*, we can calculate *precision* and *recall* at different values of ct (please refer to Appendix B for a full worked out example).

Table 4 reports the chosen metrics calculated for **Shop 1** at different values of ct; the trade-off between the two dimensions makes all the point Pareto-optimal: there is no way to increase performance in one dimension without hurting the other. Going from the first configuration ($ct = 0.996$) to the second ($ct = 0.993$) causes a big jump in the metric space, with the model losing some recall to gain *considerably* in precision. To get a sense of how the model is performing in practice, Figure 6 shows three sessions for the query "nike shoes": when session context is empty (session 1), the model defaults to the broadest category (*sneakers*); when session is *running*-based or *basketball*-based, the model adjusts its aggressiveness depending on the threshold we set. It is interesting to note that while the prediction for 2 at $ct = 0.97$ is wrong at the last node (product is *a7*, not *a3*), the model is still making a *reasonable* guess (e.g. by guessing sport and brand correctly).

In our experience, the adoption of data-driven models in traditional digital shops is often received with some skepticism over the "supervision" by business experts (Baer and Kamalnath, 2017): a common solution is to avoid the use of neural networks, in favor of model interpretability. **Session-Path**'s decision-based approach dares to dream a different dream, as the proposed architecture shows that we can retain the accuracy of deep learning and still provide a meaningful interface to business users – here, in the form of a precision/recall space to be explored with an easy-to-understand parameter.

8 Conclusions and Future Work

This research paper introduced **SessionPath**, a personalized and scalable model that dynamically suggests product paths in type-ahead systems; **Session-Path** was benchmarked on data from two shops and tested against count-based and neural models, with explicit complexity-accuracy trade-offs. Finally, we proposed a confidence-based decision rule inspired by customer discussions: by abstracting away model behavior in one parameter, we wish to solve the often hard interplay between business requirements and machine behavior; furthermore, by leveraging a hierarchical structure of product concepts, the model produces predictions that are suitable to a *prima facie* human inspection (e.g. Figure 6).

While our evaluation shows very encouraging results, the next step will be to A/B test the proposed models on a variety of target clients: **Shop 1** and **Shop 2** data comes from search logs of a last-generation search engine, which possibly skewed model behavior in subtle ways. With more data, it will be possible to extend the current work in some important directions:

1. while *this* work showed that **SessionPath** is effective, the underlying deep architecture can be improved further: on one hand, by doing more extensive optimization; on the other, by focusing on how to best perform linguistic generalization: *transfer learning* (between tasks as proposed by Skinner and Kallumadi (2019), or across clients, as described in Yu et al. (2020)) is a powerful tool that could be used to improve performances further;

Figure 6: Sample **SessionPath** predictions for the candidate query "nike shoes", with two thresholds (gray, green) and three sessions, $1, 2, 3$ (no product for session 1, a pair of running shoes for 2, a pair of basketball shoes for 3). The model reacts quickly both across sessions (switching to relevant parts of the underlying product catalog) and across threshold values, making more aggressive decisions at a lower value (green).

2. the same model can be applied with almost no changes to the search workflow, to provide a principled way to do personalized query scoping. A preliminary A/B test on **Shop 1** using the *MLP* model on a minor catalog facet yielded a small (2%) but statistically significant improvement ($p < 0.05$) on click-through rate and we look forward to extending our testing;

3. we could model path depth *within the decoder itself*, by teaching the model when to stop; as an alternative to learning a decision rule in a supervised setting, we could leverage reinforcement learning and let the system improve through iterations - in particular, the choice of cutting the path for a given query and session vector could be cast in terms of contextual bandits;

4. finally, *precision* and *recall* at different depths are just a first start; preliminary tests with *balanced accuracy* on selected examples show promising results, but we look forward to performing user studies to deepen our understanding of the ideal decision mechanism.

Personalization engines for digital shops are expected to drive an increase in profits by 15% by the end of 2020 (Gillespie et al., 2018); facet suggestions help personalizing the search experience as early as in the type-ahead drop-down window: considering that search users account globally for almost 14% of the total revenues (Charlton, 2013), and that category suggestions may improve click-through-rate and reduce cognitive load, **Session-Path** (and similar models) may play an important role in next-generation online experiences.

Acknowledgments

Thanks to (in order of appearance) Andrea Polonioli, Federico Bianchi, Ciro Greco, Piero Molino for helpful comments to previous versions of this article. We also wish to thank our anonymous reviewers, who greatly helped in improving the clarity of our exposition.

References

Himan Abdollahpouri, Robin Burke, and Bamshad Mobasher. 2017. Controlling popularity bias in learning-to-rank recommendation.

Chris Anderson. 2006. *The Long Tail: Why the Future of Business Is Selling Less of More.* Hyperion.

Tobias Baer and Vishnu Kamalnath. 2017. Controlling machine-learning algorithms and their biases.

Dzmitry Bahdanau, Kyunghyun Cho, and Yoshua Bengio. 2015. Neural machine translation by jointly learning to align and translate. *CoRR*, abs/1409.0473.

Marco Baroni, Raffaela Bernardi, and Roberto Zamparelli. 2014. Frege in space: A program of compositional distributional semantics.

Graham Charlton. 2013. Is site search less important for niche retailers?

Heng-Tze Cheng, Levent Koc, Jeremiah Harmsen, Tal Shaked, Tushar Chandra, Hrishi Aradhye, Glen Anderson, Gregory S. Corrado, Wei Chai, Mustafa Ispir, Rohan Anil, Zakaria Haque, Lichan Hong, Vihan Jain, Xiaobing Liu, and Hemal Shah. 2016. Wide & deep learning for recommender systems. In *DLRS 2016*.

Gennaro Chierchia and Sally McConnell-Ginet. 2000. *Meaning and Grammar (2nd Ed.): An Introduction to Semantics.* MIT Press, Cambridge, MA, USA.

Paul Covington, Jay Adams, and Emre Sargin. 2016. Deep neural networks for youtube recommendations. In *Proceedings of the 10th ACM Conference on Recommender Systems*, RecSys '16, page 191–198, New York, NY, USA. Association for Computing Machinery.

Jacob Devlin, Ming-Wei Chang, Kenton Lee, and Kristina Toutanova. 2019. BERT: Pre-training of deep bidirectional transformers for language understanding. In *Proceedings of the 2019 Conference of the North American Chapter of the Association for Computational Linguistics: Human Language Technologies, Volume 1 (Long and Short Papers)*, pages 4171–4186, Minneapolis, Minnesota. Association for Computational Linguistics.

Fernando Diaz, Bhaskar Mitra, and Nick Craswell. 2016. Query expansion with locally-trained word embeddings. *ArXiv*, abs/1605.07891.

Penny Gillespie, Jason Daigler, Mike Lowndes, Christina Klock, Yanna Dharmasthira, and Sandy Shen. 2018. Magic quadrant for digital commerce. Technical report, Gartner.

Laura A. Granka, Thorsten Joachims, and Geri Gay. 2004. Eye-tracking analysis of user behavior in www search. In *Proceedings of the 27th Annual International ACM SIGIR Conference on Research and Development in Information Retrieval*, SIGIR '04, page 478–479, New York, NY, USA. Association for Computing Machinery.

Mihajlo Grbovic, Nemanja Djuric, Vladan Radosavljevic, Fabrizio Silvestri, Ricardo Baeza-Yates, Andrew Feng, Erik Ordentlich, Lee Yang, and Gavin Owens. 2016. Scalable semantic matching of queries to ads in sponsored search advertising. In *Proceedings of the 39th International ACM SIGIR Conference on Research and Development in Information Retrieval*, SIGIR '16, page 375–384, New York, NY, USA. Association for Computing Machinery.

Mihajlo Grbovic, Vladan Radosavljevic, Nemanja Djuric, Narayan Bhamidipati, Jaikit Savla, Varun Bhagwan, and Doug Sharp. 2015. E-commerce in your inbox: Product recommendations at scale. In *Proceedings of KDD '15*.

Zhiwei Guan and Edward Cutrell. 2007. An eye tracking study of the effect of target rank on web search. In *Proceedings of the SIGCHI Conference on Human Factors in Computing Systems*, CHI '07, page 417–420, New York, NY, USA. Association for Computing Machinery.

Jiafeng Guo, Yixing Fan, Qingyao Ai, and W. Bruce Croft. 2016. A deep relevance matching model for ad-hoc retrieval. In *CIKM '16*.

Sheena Iyengar and Mark Lepper. 2001. When choice is demotivating: Can one desire too much of a good thing? *Journal of personality and social psychology*, 79:995–1006.

Manojkumar Rangasamy Kannadasan and Grigor Aslanyan. 2019. Personalized query autocompletion through a lightweight representation of the user context. *CoRR*, abs/1905.01386.

Saar Kuzi, Abhishek Narwekar, Anusri Pampari, and ChengXiang Zhai. 2019. Help me search: Leveraging user-system collaboration for query construction to improve accuracy for difficult queries. In *Proceedings of the 42nd International ACM SIGIR*

Conference on Research and Development in Information Retrieval, SIGIR'19, page 1221–1224, New York, NY, USA. Association for Computing Machinery.

Sonya Liberman and Ronny Lempel. 2014. Approximately optimal facet value selection. *Sci. Comput. Program.*, 94(P1):18–31.

Y. Lin, A. Datta, and G. D. Fabbrizio. 2018. E-commerce product query classification using implicit user's feedback from clicks. In *2018 IEEE International Conference on Big Data (Big Data)*, pages 1955–1959.

Tie-Yan Liu. 2009. Learning to rank for information retrieval. *Found. Trends Inf. Retr.*, 3(3):225–331.

Bernardo Magnini, Amedeo Cappelli, Emanuele Pianta, Manuela Speranza, V Bartalesi Lenzi, Rachele Sprugnoli, Lorenza Romano, Christian Girardi, and Matteo Negri. 2006. Annotazione di contenuti concettuali in un corpus italiano: I - cab. In *Proc.of SILFI 2006*.

Irina Matveeva, Chris Burges, Timo Burkard, Andy Laucius, and Leon Wong. 2006. High accuracy retrieval with multiple nested ranker. In *Proceedings of the 29th Annual International ACM SIGIR Conference on Research and Development in Information Retrieval*, SIGIR '06, page 437–444, New York, NY, USA. Association for Computing Machinery.

Tomas Mikolov, Ilya Sutskever, Kai Chen, Greg Corrado, and Jeffrey Dean. 2013a. Distributed representations of words and phrases and their compositionality. In *Proceedings of the 26th International Conference on Neural Information Processing Systems - Volume 2*, NIPS'13, pages 3111–3119, USA. Curran Associates Inc.

Tomas Mikolov, Ilya Sutskever, Kai Chen, Greg S Corrado, and Jeff Dean. 2013b. Distributed representations of words and phrases and their compositionality. In C. J. C. Burges, L. Bottou, M. Welling, Z. Ghahramani, and K. Q. Weinberger, editors, *Advances in Neural Information Processing Systems 26*, pages 3111–3119. Curran Associates, Inc.

Bhaskar Mitra and Nick Craswell. 2017. Neural models for information retrieval. *ArXiv*, abs/1705.01509.

Piero Molino, Huaixiu Zheng, and Yi-Chia Wang. 2018. Cota: Improving the speed and accuracy of customer support through ranking and deep networks. *Proceedings of the 24th ACM SIGKDD International Conference on Knowledge Discovery & Data Mining*.

Dae Hoon Park and Rikio Chiba. 2017. A neural language model for query auto-completion.

Benjamin Scheibehenne, Rainer Greifeneder, and Peter M. Todd. 2010. Can There Ever Be Too Many Options? A Meta-Analytic Review of Choice Overload. *Journal of Consumer Research*, 37(3):409–425.

Michael Skinner. 2018. Product categorization with lstms and balanced pooling views. In *eCOM@SIGIR*.

Michael Skinner and Surya Kallumadi. 2019. E-commerce query classification using product taxonomy mapping: A transfer learning approach. In *eCOM@SIGIR*.

Jacopo Tagliabue and Reuben Cohn-Gordon. 2019. Lexical learning as an online optimal experiment: Building efficient search engines through human-machine collaboration. *ArXiv*, abs/1910.14164.

Damir Vandic, Flavius Frasincar, and Uzay Kaymak. 2013. Facet selection algorithms for web product search. In *Proceedings of the 22nd ACM International Conference on Information & Knowledge Management*, CIKM '13, page 2327–2332, New York, NY, USA. Association for Computing Machinery.

Cheng Wang, Mathias Niepert, and Hui Li. 2018a. LRMM: Learning to recommend with missing modalities. In *Proceedings of the 2018 Conference on Empirical Methods in Natural Language Processing*, pages 3360–3370, Brussels, Belgium. Association for Computational Linguistics.

Po-Wei Wang et al. 2018b. Realtime query completion via deep language models. In *eCOM@SIGIR*, volume 2319 of *CEUR Workshop Proceedings*. CEUR-WS.org.

Ronald J. Williams and David Zipser. 1989. A learning algorithm for continually running fully recurrent neural networks.

Bingqing Yu, Jacopo Tagliabue, Federico Bianchi, and Ciro Greco. 2020. An image is worth a thousand features: Scalable product representations for in-session type-ahead personalization. In *Companion Proceedings of the Web Conference*, New York, NY, USA. Association for Computing Machinery.

Barret Zoph and Quoc V. Le. 2016. Neural architecture search with reinforcement learning. *ArXiv*, abs/1611.01578.

A Architectural Considerations

Figure 7 represents a functional overview of a type-ahead service: when *User X* on a shop starts typing a query after browsing some products, the query seed and the session context are sent to the server. An existing engine - traditional or neural - will then take the query and the context and produce a list of top-k query candidates, ranked by relevance, which are then sent back to the client to populate the dropdown window of the search bar.

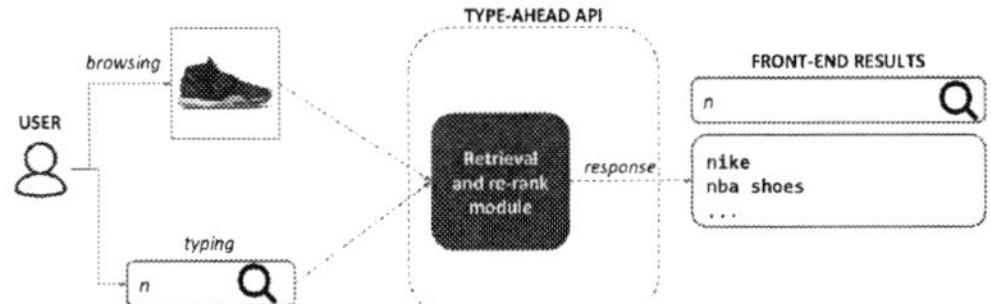

Figure 7: High-level functional overview of an industry standard API for type-ahead suggestions: query seed and possibly session information about the user are sent by the client to the server, where some retrieval and re-ranking module produces the final top-k suggestions and prepares the response for front-end consumption.

As depicted in Figure 8, category suggestions can be quickly added to any existing infrastructure by treating the current engine as a "black-box" and adding path predictions at run-time for the first (or the first k, since requests to the model at that point can be batched with little overhead) query candidate(s). In this scenario, the decoupling between retrieval and suggestions is absolute, which may be a good idea when the stacks are very different (say, traditional retrieval *and* neural suggestions), but less extreme solutions are obviously possible. The crucial engineering point is that path prediction (using any of the methods from Section 7) can be added and tested quickly, with few conceptual and engineering dependencies: the more traditional the existing stack, the more an incremental approach is recommended: count-based first - since predictions can be served simply from an in-memory map -, **MLP** second - since predictions require a small neural network, but they are fast enough to only require CPU at query time -, and finally the full **SessionPath** - which requires dedicated hardware considerations to be effective in the time constraints of the type-ahead use case. As a practical suggestion, we also found quite effective when using simpler models (e.g. **MLP**) to first test it at a *given depth*: for example, you start by only classifying the most likely nodes in template *sport / ?*, and then incrementally increase the target classes by adding more diverse paths.

Adding a lightweight wrapper around the original bare-bone endpoint allows for other improvements as well: for example, considering typical power-law of query logs, a caching layer can be used to avoid a full retrieving-and-rerank iteration for frequent queries; obviously, this and similar features are independent from **SessionPath** itself.

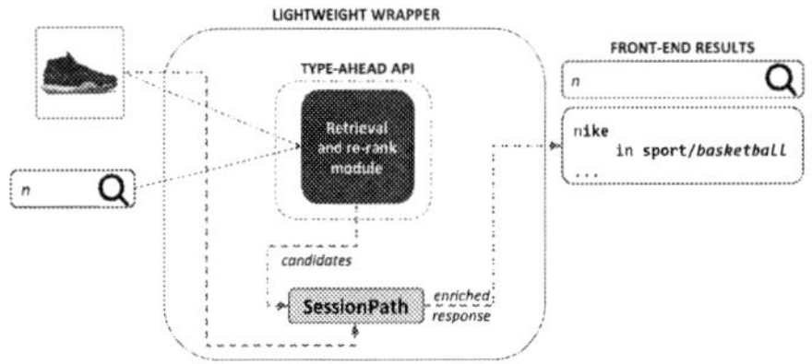

Figure 8: A lightweight **SessionPath** functional integration: starting from a standard flow (Figure 7, a simple wrapper around the existing module sends the same session information and the top-n suggestions to **SessionPath**, for dynamic path prediction. The final response is then obtained by simply augmenting the existing response containing query candidates with category predictions.

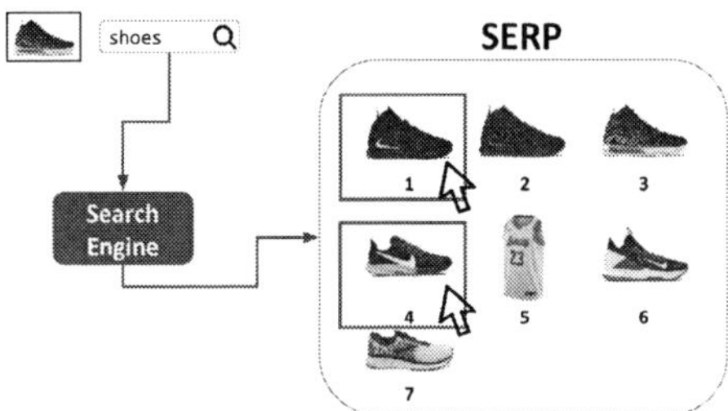

Figure 9: A sample row in the test set, displaying search results (7 products in 4 paths) for the query "shoes" and a session containing a pair of *LeBron James* basketball shoes. In this example, the shopper clicked on products P_1 and P_4.

B Metrics Calculation: a Worked-Out Example

For the sake of reproducibility, we present a worked out example of metrics calculations for offline testing of the decision module (Section 7.2). Figure 9 depicts an historical interaction from the search logs: a session containing a product, a query issued by the user and the search result page ("serp"), containing seven items belonging to the following paths:

$P_1 = sport / basketball / lebron$
$P_2 = sport / basketball / lebron$
$P_3 = sport / basketball / lebron$
$P_4 = sport / running / sneakers$
$P_5 = sport / basketball / jerseys$
$P_6 = sport / basketball / curry$
$P_7 = sport / running / sneakers.$

Click-through data (i.e. products in the serp clicked by the user) indicates that P_1 and P_4 are relevant, and so the associated paths are ground truths (*sport/basketball/lebron* and *sport/running/sneakers*). We now present the full calculations in three scenarios, corresponding to three level of depths in the predicted path.

Scenario 1 (general): prediction is *sport*. In this case, result set would be intact, so: *True Positives* (**TP**) are P_1, P_2, P_3, P_4, P_7, *False Positives* (**FP**) are P_5, P_6, *False Negatives* (**FN**) are $\emptyset$. *Precision* is: **TP** / (**TP** + **FP**) $= 5/(5+2) = 0.71$, *Recall* is: **TP** / (**TP** + **FN**) $= 5/(5+0) = 1.0$ (with no cut, all truths are retrieved so 1.0 is the expected result).

Scenario 2 (intermediate): prediction is *sport/basketball*. In this case, filtering the result set according to the decision made by the model would give P_1, P_2, P_3, P_5, P_6 as the final set. So: **TP** $= P_1, P_2, P_3$, **FP** $= P_5, P_6$, **FN** $= P_4, P_7$; *Precision* $= 3/(3+2) = 0.6$, *Recall* $= 3/(3+2) = 0.6$.

Scenario 3 (specific): prediction is *sport / basketball / lebron*. In this case, filtering the result set according to the decision made by the model would give P_1, P_2, P_3 as the final set. So: **TP** $= P_1, P_2, P_3$, **FP** $= \emptyset$, **FN** $= P_4, P_7$; *Precision* $= 3/(3+0) = 1.0$, *Recall* $= 3/(3+2) = 0.6$.

The full calculations show very clearly the natural trade-off discussed at length in Section 7.2: the deeper the path, the more precise are the results but also the higher the chance of hiding valuable products from the shopper.

Deep Learning-based Online Alternative Product Recommendations at Scale

Mingming Guo, Nian Yan, Xiquan Cui, San He Wu, Unaiza Ahsan,
Rebecca West and Khalifeh Al Jadda

The Home Depot, Atlanta, GA, USA

{mingming_guo, nian_yan, xiquan_cui, san_h_wu, unaiza_ahsan,
rebecca_west, khalifeh_al_jadda}@homedepot.com

Abstract

Alternative recommender systems are critical for ecommerce companies. They guide customers to explore a massive product catalog and assist customers to find the right products among an overwhelming number of options. However, it is a non-trivial task to recommend alternative products that fit customers' needs. In this paper, we use both textual product information (e.g. product titles and descriptions) and customer behavior data to recommend alternative products. Our results show that the coverage of alternative products is significantly improved in offline evaluations as well as recall and precision. The final A/B test shows that our algorithm increases the conversion rate by 12% in a statistically significant way. In order to better capture the semantic meaning of product information, we build a Siamese Network with Bidirectional LSTM to learn product embeddings. In order to learn a similarity space that better matches the preference of real customers, we use co-compared data from historical customer behavior as labels to train the network. In addition, we use NMSLIB to accelerate the computationally expensive kNN computation for millions of products so that the alternative recommendation is able to scale across the entire catalog of a major ecommerce site.

1 Introduction

Recommender systems are pervasive in ecommerce and other web systems (Zhang et al. 2019). Alternative product recommendation is an important way to help customers easily find the right products and speed up their buying decision process. For example, if a customer is viewing a "25.5 cu. ft. Counter Depth French Door Refrigerator in Stainless Steel", she may also be interested in other french door refrigerators in different brands but with similar features such as capacity, counter depth, material, etc.

There are two main ways to obtain an alternative product list for a given product. First is a content-based recommendation approach. If two products have similar attributes or content so that one can be replaced by the other, we can consider them as alternative products. Word2vec has been used to learn item embeddings for comparing item similarities (Caselles-Dupre, Lesaint, and Royo-Letelier 2018). However, this unsupervised learning process does not guarantee the embedding distance is consistent with customers' shopping preference. The second way is to leverage customer behavior to find alternative products in the style of item-to-item collaborative filtering (Linden, Smith, and York 2003). If customers frequently consider two products together, one product can be recommended as an alternative for the other. Unfortunately, this approach has a cold start problem.

In this work, we formulate the recommendation problem into a supervised product embedding learning process. To be specific, we develop a deep learning based embedding approach using Siamese Network, which leverages both product content (including title and description) and customer behavior to generate Top-N recommendations for an anchor product. Our contributions are as follows:

- Recommend alternative products using both product textual information and customer behavior data. This allows us to better handle both the cold start and relevancy problems.

- Use a Bidirectional LSTM structure to better capture the semantic meaning of product textual information.

- Build a Siamese Network to incorporate co-compared customer behavior data to guide the supervised learning process and generate a product embedding space that better matches customer's preference.

- Our model outperforms baselines in both offline validations and an online A/B test.

Proceedings of the 3rd Workshop on e-Commerce and NLP (ECNLP 3), pages 19–23
Online, July 10, 2020. ©2020 Association for Computational Linguistics

2 Problem Formulation

We have the textual information $T = \{x_1, ..., x_N\}$ (a concatenation of product title and description) of a catalog of products $P = \{p_1, ..., p_N\}$ to make recommendations. The goal of the alternative recommendation is to learn a embedding projection function f_w so that the embedding of an anchor product that is viewed by a customer $f_w(x_a)$ is close to the embeddings of its alternatives $f_w(x_r)$. In this paper, we use the cosine similarity between the embeddings of $f_w(x_a)$ and $f_w(x_r)$ as the energy function.

$$E_w = \frac{\langle f_w(x_a), f_w(x_r) \rangle}{\|f_w(x_a)\| \|f_w(x_r)\|} \quad (1)$$

The problem is how to learn a function as the embedding projection function f_w to better capture the semantic meanings of the product textual information and project a sequence of tokens x_i into an embedding vector of size d. The total loss over the training data set $X = \left\{ x_a^{(i)}, x_r^{(i)}, y^{(i)} \right\}$ is given by

$$L_w(X) = \sum_{i=1}^{M} L_w^{(i)}(x_a^{(i)}, x_r^{(i)}, y^{(i)}) \quad (2)$$

where the instance loss function $L_w^{(i)}$ is a contrastive loss function. It consists of a term L_+ for the positive cases ($y^{(i)} = 1$), where the product pair are alternative to each other. In addition, it consists of a term L_- for the negative cases ($y^{(i)} = 0$), where the product pair are not often considered together by customers.

$$L_w^{(i)} = y^{(i)} L_+\left(x_a^{(i)}, x_r^{(i)}\right) + (1 - y^{(i)}) L_-(x_a^{(i)}, x_r^{(i)}) \quad (3)$$

The loss functions for the positive and negative cases are given by:

$$L_+\left(x_a^{(i)}, x_r^{(i)}\right) = |1 - E_w| \quad (4)$$

$$L_-\left(x_a^{(i)}, x_r^{(i)}\right) = \begin{cases} |E_w| & if\ E_w > 0 \\ 0 & otherwise \end{cases} \quad (5)$$

Based on the loss function, the problem is how to build a network that can learn part of the product information that is important for customers and project a product to the right embedding space that is consistent with customers' preference.

3 Deep Learning Embedding Approach

Textual Data and Co-compared Data

Product Information: From the ecommerce site catalog data, we extract the product ID, product title and description as the raw textual data with an example in Table 1.

Product ID	Product Title	Product Description
'12345678'	60 Gal. Electric Air Compressor	This compressor offers a solid cast iron, twin cylinder compressor pump for extreme durability. It also offers 135 psi maximum pressure and air delivery 11.5/10.2 SCFM at 40/90 psi.

Table 1. Product Textual Data

Co-compared Data: Customers can select several products on a search result page for co-comparison to verify how they are similar and different based on their features. Those products are considered alternative to each other. The co-compared is a strong signal of the similarity between products within same product taxonomy. We extract co-compared data from clickstream to create the training data. Some examples of the co-compared data are shown in Table 2.

Product ID	Product ID	Co-compared
'12345678'	'87654321'	1
'32187654'	'54321876'	1

Table 2. Co-compared Example

Siamese Network with Bidirectional LSTM

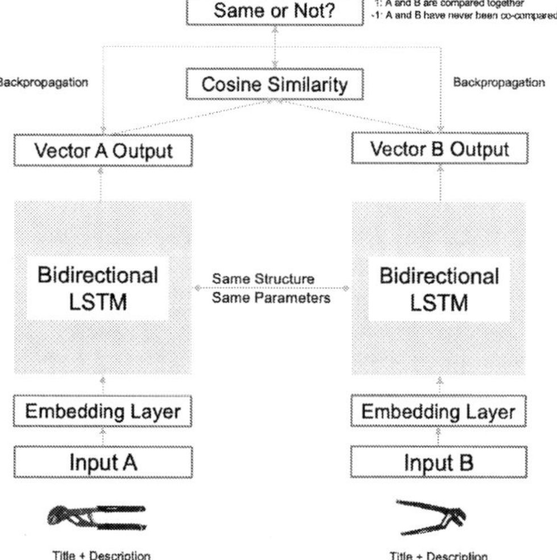

Fig. 1 Siamese Network with Bidirectional LSTM

We build a Siamese Network (Bromley et al. 1994) with Bidirectional LSTM (Graves and Schmidhuber 2005) components to learn and generate embeddings for all products. The product embedding space better captures the semantic meaning of the product textural information and customer preferences. Textual data are in a sequential format and the order of the texts matters for the network. We choose Bidirectional LSTM to learn representation in both directions from the input sequences. We use Keras with TensorFlow to build and train the network. We choose RMSprop (Hinton et al. 2012) as the optimizer. The loss function is the binary cross entropy. The network architecture is shown in Figure 1.

Creating Training Data by Sampling

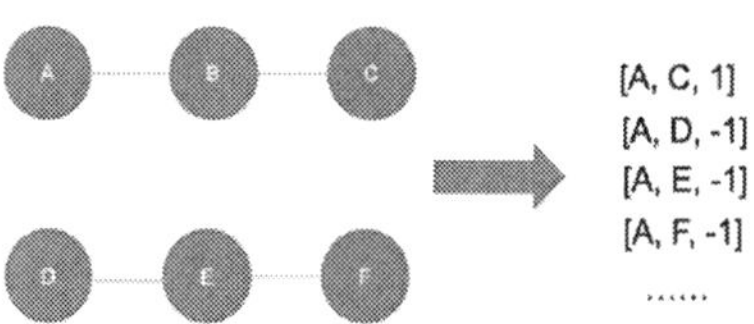

Fig. 2 Connected Graphs

Positive and negative sampling: we filter out the products without titles and/or descriptions from the co-compared data. We form a connected graph from the co-compared product pairs. For example, if product A and B are co-compared and product B and C are co-compared, then (A, B, C) forms a connected graph. If products D and E are co-compared and E and F are co-compared, then (D, E, F) forms a connection graph. We create positive samples for each product by randomly sampling another product within the same set, e.g. [A, C, 1]. We also create negative samples for each product in a connected graph by randomly sampling a different connected graph first, then randomly sampling a product in that graph, e.g. [A, D, -1], as shown in Figure 2.

How many data points	How many products	What's the time period (year)
331900	65684	1

Table 3. Training Data Statistics

The negative sampling space is much larger than the positive sampling space because only a small number of products are frequently co-compared together by our customers. Thus, for each anchor product, we sample more negative samples than positive samples. Based on our experiments and empirically analysis, for each

positive sample, three negative samples are created which gives the best performance on the validation loss when training the model. The statistics of the training data is shown in Table 3.

Training the Model and Generating Embeddings

The Siamese Network training process takes about 10 hours to converge. The next step is to load the best model weights to generate product embeddings. Specifically, from the Siamese Network, we remove the last cosine similarity layer and the second input branch which processes the second product of the product pairs. We only use the Embedding layer and the Bidirectional LSTM layer. The final result is the concatenation of the hidden state of the product title and the hidden state of the product description.

Scalable Recommendation Generation

We generate millions of embeddings based on product titles and descriptions. For each product, the task is to compute distances with the rest of millions of product embeddings using a similarity metric, e.g. cosine similarity, and rank the similarity scores from higher to lower to get the Top-N recommended products. According to the detailed analysis from (Aumüller et al. 2019), we choose NMSLIB (Boytsov et al. 2016) library to conduct heavy kNN computations because it has high performance in both recall and queries per second.

4 Performance Evaluation

In this section, we describe how we evaluate the effectiveness and efficiency of our deep learning model with offline evaluation and online A/B test. We use our production data to validate the results since this is a unique case for us. We did not find exact similar open data set with similar customer behaviors that can be used for our evaluation.

Algorithms:

1) Baseline 1: Attributed Based

This baseline algorithm uses product attributes to generate recommendations. The attributes contain numerical and categorical data. The categorical features are converted into numerical format using one-hot encoding. The distance between two products is computed using cosine similarity. This is the content-based method we compare with.

2) Baseline 2: Frequently Compared

This baseline algorithm uses the actual customer co-compared data. The recommendations are ranked by the co-comparison counts. Due to the cold-start problem, many products in the catalog do not have such recommendations even we create labels from the co-compared data. This is the collaborative filtering method we compare with since it's based on item-to-item relationships built by customer browsing behaviors.

3) Proposed: Deep Learning Based

For Deep Learning Based, we choose 0.8 as the cutting threshold for the cosine similarity score. This threshold is selected and validated based on the judgement from our human expert validators after they examine thousands of random sampled anchors from the catalog data and the recommendations generated from our model. We only keep the recommendations that have at least 0.8 similarity with each anchor product.

Offline Evaluation:

1) Precision and Recall:

	Precision			Recall		
	Top 1	Top 5	Top 10	Top 1	Top 5	Top 10
Attribute Based	0.23%	0.13%	0.10%	0.15%	0.34%	0.33%
Frequently Compared	0.75%	0.51%	0.47%	0.51%	0.93%	1.02%
Deep Learning Based	1.47%	0.81%	0.61%	0.91%	2.08%	2.59%

Table 4. Precision and Recall

Comparison 1:

Two weeks of actual customer purchase data from clickstream data is used to evaluate the performance of all 3 algorithms based on precision and recall. There are total 1.1 million purchase sessions. In this comparison, we use the raw data regardless if each session has all two baselines. This is a fair comparison since not all anchors can be covered by both algorithms. For example, a product may not have the same set of attributes as other products so this product cannot be covered by Attributed Based algorithm. This is because there are vast variants of similar products without same set of attributes. Another scenario is that this product has never been compared with other products by our customers so this product cannot be covered by Frequently Compared algorithm. For the Deep Learning Based, we compare its recommendations with the purchased items. Table 4 shows our algorithm performs much better than the baseline algorithms for all top 1, 5, and 10 items precision and recall scores, especially for

precision top 1, recall top 5 and top 10. The main reasons are: i) Frequently Compared recommends co-compared products by customers and only covers small sets of products; ii) Attributed Based approach has a higher coverage but a lower relevancy.

Comparison 2:

In this comparison, we select sessions that have both Attributed Based and Frequently Compared. Table 5 shows our Deep Learning Based still performs much better than Attributed Based but not Frequently Compared. The reason is that the label we used to train our model is from co-compared data, so our model has the upbound from Frequently Compared's performance. This experiment validated our hypothesis.

	Precision			Recall		
	Top 1	Top 5	Top 10	Top 1	Top 5	Top 10
Attribute Based	0.21%	0.13%	0.12%	0.16%	0.31%	0.34%
Frequently Compared	**2.48%**	**1.81%**	**1.75%**	**1.65%**	**2.65%**	2.76%
Deep Learning Based	1.72%	0.90%	0.67%	1.09%	2.33%	**2.85%**

Table 5. Precision and Recall

2) Coverage: The anchor coverages of all the algorithms are also computed. The Attributes Based and Frequently Compared approaches cover 31.5% and 47.1% of anchors, respectively, and those two numbers are increased to 81.2% and 83.4% with the incremental increase from our Deep Learning Based approach. Since most of our products have titles and descriptions, so our Deep Learning Based significantly boosts the coverage of anchor products from our catalog to have good recommendations.

Online A/B Testing:

Conversion Rate: The A/B test was run for three weeks and success was measured using conversion rate. Conversion rate is the number of purchases divided by number of visits which captures the similarity between anchor and recommendations. Our deep learning model outperforms the existing hybrid algorithm which combined Attribute Based and Frequently Compared with a **12%** higher conversion rate. This is a very successful test for our business. We're implementing the deep learning algorithm on our production site.

5   Related Work

The traditional method for recommender systems is content-based recommendations (Lops et al. 2011). This method can handle the cold start problem well. Collaborative Filtering is another method based on user behaviors. For example, Matrix Factorization (Koren et al. 2009) is a widely used method for collaborative filtering. Our two baseline algorithms, one is considered as content-based and the other is considered as collaborative filtering using user behavior data with the co-compared format. Deep learning now has been widely used not only in the academic community, but also in industrial recommender system settings, such as Airbnb's listing recommendations (Grbovic and Cheng 2018) and Pinterest's recommendation engine (Ying et al. 2018). Most of recent deep learning papers (e.g., Wang et al. 2019; Ebesu, Shen, and Fang 2018) have been focused on sequential recommendations. (Neculoiu et al. 2016) presents a deep network using Siamese architecture with character-level Bidirectional LSTM for job title normalization. (Mueller and Thyagarajan 2016) also presents a Siamese adaptation of the LSTM to learn sentence embedding. However, this work needs human annotated labels while our labels are extracted from clickstream data. Our work more focuses on providing alternative recommendations by learning product embedding from product textual data and customer signals.

6   Conclusion

Recommender Systems are core functions for online retailers to increase their revenue. To help customers easily find alternative products in an automated way, we develop a deep learning approach to generate product embeddings based on a Siamese Network with Bidirectional LSTM. We extract co-compared data from customer clickstream and product textual data to train the network and generate the embedding space. Our approach significantly improves the coverage of similar products as well as improving recall and precision. Our algorithm also shows promising results on conversion rate in an online A/B test.

References

Aumüller, M.; Bernhardsson, E.; Faithfull, A. 2019. ANN-Benchmarks: A Benchmarking Tool for Approximate Nearest Neighbor Algorithms. *Information Systems*.

Boytsov, L.; Novak, D.; Malkov, Y.; Nyberg, E. 2016. Off the Beaten Path: Let's Replace Term-Based Retrieval with k-NN Search. In *proceedings of CIKM*.

Bromley, J.; Guyon, I.; LeCun, Y.; Sackinger, E.; and Shah, R. 1994. Signature verification using a "Siamese" time delay neural network. In *Proceedings of Advances in Neural Information Processing Systems*, 737-744.

Caselles-Dupre, H.; Lesaint, F.; and Royo-Letelier, J. 2018. Word2vec applied to recommendation: hyperparameters matter. In *Proceedings of RecSys*, 352-356.

Ebesu, T.; Shen, B.; and Fang, Y. 2018. Collaborative memory network for recommendation systems. In *Proceedings of SIGIR*, 515-524.

Graves, A. and Schmidhuber, J. 2005. Framewise phoneme classification with Bidirectional LSTM and other neural network architectures. In *Proceedings of IEEE International Join Conference on Neural Networks*, July 31-Aug 4.

Grbovic, M. and Cheng, H. 2018. Real-time personalization using embeddings for search ranking at Airbnb. In *Proc. Of the 24th ACM SIGKDD International Conference on Knowledge Discovery & Data Mining*, 311-320.

Hinton, G.; Srivastava, N.; and Swersky, K. 2012. Neural networks for machine learning lecture 6a overview of mini-batch gradient descent.

Keras, the python deep learning library: http://keras.io.

Koren, Y.; Bell, R.; and Volinsky C. 2009. Matrix factorization techniques for recommender systems. In *Proceedings of IEEE Computer*, Vol. 42, No. 8, 30-37.

Linden, G.; Smith, B.; and York, J. 2003. Amazon.com Recommendations: Item-to-Item Collaborative Filtering. In *IEEE Internet Computing*, Vol. 7, Issue 1, 76-80.

Lops, P.; Gemmis, M. de; and Semeraro, G. 2011. Content-based recommender systems: state of the art and trends. In *Recommender Systems Handbook*, 73-100.

Wang, X.; He, X.; Wang, M.; Feng, F.; and Chua T.S. 2019. Neural graph collaborative filtering. In *Proceedings of SIGIR*, July 21-25.

Ying, R.; He, R.; Chen, K.; Eksombatchai, P.; Hamilton W. L.; and Leskovec, J. 2018. Graph convolutional neural networks for web-scale recommender systems. In *24th SIGKDD*, 974-983.

Zhang, S.; Yao, L.; Sun, A.; Tay, Y. 2019. Deep learning based recommender system: a survey and new perspectives. In *Journal of ACM Computing Surveys (CSUR)*, Vol 52, Issue 1, No. 5.

A Deep Learning System for
Sentiment Analysis of Service Calls

Yanan Jia

Businessolver / Bellevue, WA

`yjia@businessolver.com`

Abstract

Sentiment analysis is crucial for the advancement of artificial intelligence (AI). Sentiment understanding can help AI to replicate human language and discourse. Studying the formation and response of sentiment state from well-trained Customer Service Representatives (CSRs) can help make the interaction between humans and AI more intelligent.

In this paper, a sentiment analysis pipeline is first carried out with respect to real-world multi-party conversations - that is, service calls. Based on the acoustic and linguistic features extracted from the source information, a novel aggregated method for voice sentiment recognition framework is built. Each party's sentiment pattern during the communication is investigated along with the interaction sentiment pattern between all parties.

1   Introduction

The natural reference for AI systems is human behavior. In human social life, emotional intelligence is important for successful and effective communication. Humans have the natural ability to comprehend and react to the emotions of their communication partners through vocal and facial expressions (Kotti and Paternò, 2012; Poria et al., 2014a). A long-standing goal of AI has been to create affective agents that can recognize, interpret and express emotions.

Early-stage research in affective computing and sentiment analysis has mainly focused on understanding affect towards entities such as movie, product, service, candidacy, organization, action and so on in monologues, which involves only one person's opinion. However, with the advent of Human-Robot Interaction (HRI) such as voice assistants and customer service chatbots, researchers have started to build empathetic dialogue systems to improve the overall HRI experience by adapting to customers' sentiment.

Sentiment study of Human-Human Interactions (HHI) can help machines identify and react to human non-verbal communication which makes the HRI experience more natural. The call center is a rich resource of communication data. A large number of calls are recorded daily in order to assess the quality of interactions between CSRs and customers. Learning the sentiment expressions from well-trained CSRs during communication can help AI understand not only what the user says, but also how he/she says it so that the interaction feels more human.

In this paper, we target and use real-world data - service calls, which poses additional challenges with respect to the artificial datasets that have been typically used in the past in multimodal sentiment researches (Cambria et al., 2017), such as variability and noises. The basic 'sentiment' can be described on a scale of approval or disapproval, good or bad, positive or negative, and termed polarity (Poria et al., 2014b).

In the service industry, the key task is to enhance the quality of services by identifying issues that may be caused by systems of rules, or service qualities. These issues are usually expressed by a caller's anger or disappointment on a call. In addition, service chatbots are widely used to answer customer calls. If customers get angry during HRI, the system should be able to transfer the customers to a live agent. In this study, we mainly focuses on identifying 'negative' sentiment, especially 'angry' customers. Given the non-homogeneous nature of full call recordings, which typically include a mixture of negative, and nonnegative statements, sentiment analysis is addressed at the sentence level. Call segments are explored in both acoustic and linguistic modalities. The temporal sentiment patterns between customers and CSRs appearing in calls are described.

The paper is organized as follows: Section 2 covers a brief literature review on sentiment recognition

Proceedings of the 3rd Workshop on e-Commerce and NLP (ECNLP 3), pages 24–34
Online, July 10, 2020. ©2020 Association for Computational Linguistics

from different modalities; Section 3 proposes a pipeline which features our novelties in training data creation using real-world multi-party conversations, including a description of the data acquisition, speaker diarization, transcription, and semi-supervised learning annotation; the methodologies for acoustic and linguistic sentiment analysis are presented in Section 4; Section 5 illustrates the methodologies adopted for fusing different modalities; Section 6 presents experimental results including the evaluation measures and temporal sentiment patterns; finally, Section 7 concludes the paper and outlines future work.

2 Related Work

In this section, we provide a brief overview of related work about text-based and audio-based sentiment analysis.

2.1 Text-based Sentiment Analysis

Sentiment analysis has focused primarily on the processing of text and mainly consists of either rule-based classifiers that make use of large sentiment lexicons, or data-driven methods that assume the availability of a large annotated corpora.

Sentiment lexicon is a list of lexical features (e.g. words) which are generally labeled according to their semantic orientation as either positive or negative (Liu, 2010). Widely used lexicons include binary polarity-based lexicons, such as Harvard General Inquirer (Stone et al., 1966), Linguistic Inquiry and Word Count (LIWC, pronounced 'Luke') (Pennebaker et al., 2007, 2001), Bing (Liu, 2012), and valence-based lexicons, such as AFINN (Nielsen, 2011), SentiWordNet (Alhazmi et al., 2013), and SnticNet (Cambria et al., 2010). Employing these lexical, researchers can apply their own rules or use existing rule-based modeling, such as VADER (Hutto and Gilbert, 2015), to do sentiment analysis. One big advantage for the rule-based models is that these approaches require no training data and generalize to multiple domains. However, since words are annotated based on their context-free semantic orientation, word-sense disambiguation (Hutto and Gilbert, 2015) may occur when the word has multiple meanings. For example, words like 'defeated', 'envious', and 'stunned' are classified as 'positive' in Bing, but '-2' (negative) in AFINN. Although the rule-based algorithm is known to be noisy and limited, a sentiment lexicon is a useful component for any sophisticated sentiment detection algorithm

and is one of the main resources to start from (Poria et al., 2014b).

Another major line of work in sentiment analysis consists of data-driven methods based on a large dataset annotated for polarity. The most widely used datasets include the MPQA corpus which is a collection of manually annotated news articles (Wiebe et al., 2005; Wilson et al., 2005), movie reviews with two polarity (Pang and Lee, 2004a), a collection of newspaper headlines annotated for polarity (Strapparava and Mihalcea, 2007). With a large annotated datasets, supervised classifiers have been applied (Go et al., 2009; Pang and Lee, 2004b; dos Santos and Gatti, 2014; Socher et al., 2013; Wang et al., 2016). Such approaches step away from blind use of keywords and word co-occurrence count, but rather rely on the implicit features associated with large semantic knowledge bases (Cambria et al., 2015).

2.2 Audio-based Sentiment Analysis

Vocal expression is a primary carrier of affective signals in human communication. Speech as signals contains several features that can extract linguistic, speaker-specific information, and emotional. Related work about audio-based sentiment analysis along with multimodal fusion is reviewed in this section.

Studies on speech-based sentiment analysis have focused on identifying relevant acoustic features. Use open source software such as OpenEAR (Eyben et al., 2009), openSMILE (Eyben et al., 2010), JAudio toolkit (McEnnis et al., 2005) or library packages (McFee et al., 2015; Sueur et al., 2008) to extract features. These features along with some of their statistical derivates are closely related to the vocal prosodic characteristics, such as a tone, a volume, a pitch, an intonation, an inflection, a duration, etc.

Supervised or unsupervised classifiers can be fitted based on the statistical derivates of these features (Jain et al., 2018; Pan et al., 2012). Sequence models can be fitted based on filter banks, Mel-frequency cepstral coefficients (MFCCs), or other low-level descriptors extracted from raw speech without feature engineering (Aguilar et al., 2019). However, this approach usually requires highly efficient computation and large annotated audio files. Multimodal sentiment analysis has started to draw attention recently because of the unlimited multimodality source of information online, such as videos and audios (Cambria et al., 2017; Poria, 2016; Poria et al., 2015). Most of the multimodal sentiment analysis is focused on monologue videos. In the last few years, sentiment recognition in conversations has started to gain research interest, since reproducing human interaction requires a deep understanding of conversations, and sentiment plays a pivotal role in conversations. The existing conversation datasets are usually recorded in a controlled environment, such as a lab, and segmented into utterances, transcribe to text and annotated with emotion or sentiment labels manually. Widely used datasets include AMI Meeting Corpus (Carletta et al., 2006), IEMOCAP (Busso et al., 2008), SEMAINE (Mckeown et al., 2013) and AVEC (Schuller et al., 2012).

Recently, a few recurrent neural network (RNN) models are developed for emotion detection in conversations, e.g. DialogueRNN (Majumder et al., 2019) or ICON(Hazarika et al., 2018). However they are less accurate in emotion detection for the utterances with emotional shift (Poria et al., 2019) and the training data requires the speaker information. The conversation models are not employed in our polarity sentiment analysis because of the quality of the data and the approach used to gain the training data. More detailed explanations can be found in Section 3.4.

At the heart of any multimodal sentiment analysis engine is the multimodal fusion (Shan et al., 2007; Zeng et al., 2007). The multimodal fusion integrates all single modalities into a combined single representation. Features are extracted from each modality of the data independently. Decision-level fusion feeds the features of each modality into separate classifiers and then combines their decisions. Feature-level fusion concatenates the feature vectors obtained from all modalities and feeds the resulting long vector into a supervised classifier. Recent research on multimodal fusion for sentiment recognition has been conducted at either the feature level or decision level (Poria, 2016; Poria et al., 2015).

3   Dataset and Pipeline

The data resources used for our experiments are described in Section 3.1. Data preparation including speech transcription and speaker diarization is discussed in Section 3.2. The sentiment annotation guideline is introduced in Section 3.3. Section 3.4 presents a semi-supervised learning annotation pipeline that chains data preparation, model training, model deploying and data monitor.

3.1   BSCD: Benefits Service Call Dataset

The main dataset we created in this paper consists of service calls collected from a health care benefits Call Center (named BSCD). Calls are focused on customers looking for help or support with company provided benefits such as health insurance. 500 calls are collected from the call center database covering diverse topics, such as insurance plan information, insurance id card, dependent coverage, etc. The call dataset has female and male speakers randomly selected with their age ranging approximately from 16-80. Calls involving translators are eliminated to keep only speakers expressing themselves in English. All the calls are presented in Wave format with a sample rate of 8000 Hertz and duration varying from 4 minutes to 26 minutes. All calls are pre-processed to eliminate repetitive introductions. The beginning of each call contains an introduction of the users' company name by a robot. To address this issue, the segment before the first pause (silence duration > 1 second) is removed from each call.

A robust computational model of sentiment analysis needs to be able to handle real-world variability and noises. While the previous researches on multimodal sentiment or emotion analysis use audio and visual recorded in laboratory settings (Busso et al., 2008; Mckeown et al., 2010, 2013); the BSCD gathers real-world calls which contain ambient noise present in most audio recordings, as well as diversity in person-to-person communication patterns. Both of these conditions result in difficulties that need to be addressed in order to effectively extract useful data from these sources.

3.2   Data Preparation

To discard noise and long pauses (silence duration > 5 seconds) in calls, Voice Activity Detection (VAD) is applied, followed by the application of Automatic Speech Recognition (ASR) and Automatic Speaker Diarization (ASD) to transcribe the verbal statements, extract the start and end time of each utterance, and identify the speaker of each utterance. Each call is segmented into an average of 69 utterances. The duration of the utterances is right-skewed with a median of 2.9 seconds; first and third quantiles 1.6 and 5.1 seconds.

By searching keywords such as 'How can I help' in the content of each utterance, speakers are labeled

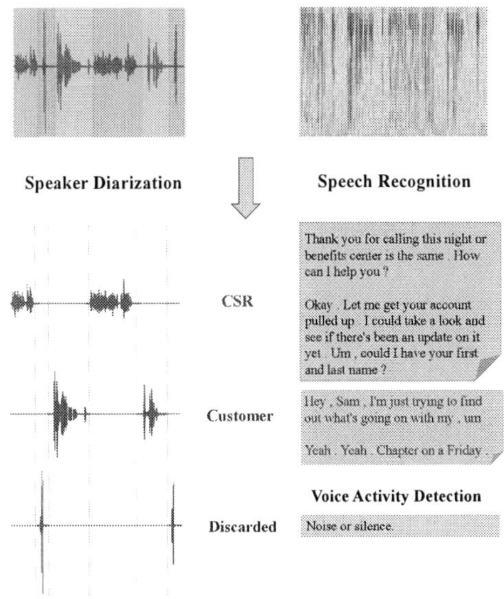

Figure 1: Data preparation workflow

as CSR or customer. Each utterance is linked to the corresponding audio stream, auto transcription, as well as speaker label. The workflow and corresponding results for the first 23 seconds of one selected call are shown in Figure 1, where the original input is a call audio sample. After data preparation, segments of noise and silence are discarded. This call sample is segmented into 4 utterances. The audio streams are from the original audio and split based on the start and end time of each utterance. Auto transcriptions are more likely to be ungrammatical if the recording quality is bad or the conversation contains words that ASR cannot identify or the speakers do not express themselves clearly. The ungrammatical transcriptions usually occur in customer parts and the frequency of ungrammaticality varies from case to case. Although the sentiment recognition of a whole call tends to be robust with respect to speech recognition errors, the sensitivity of each utterance analysis to ASR errors is not reparable given our study. The speaker labels are from ASD output which can be misclassified because of the occurrence of speakers overlapping or speakers with similar acoustic features. Conversation sentiment pattern study can be misleading due to the misclassified ASD output, although misclassified ASD is rare.

This process allows us to study features from both modalities: transcribed words and acoustics. Distinguishing different parties gives us the ability to study the temporal sentiment transitions of individ-

ual speakers and interactions among speakers in a conversation. However, since the data preparation is part of the pipeline described in section 3.4, which runs in real-time, sentiment analysis must rely on error-prone ASR and ASD outputs.

3.3 Sentiment Annotation

Sentiment annotation is a challenging task as the label depends on the annotators' perspective, and the differences inherent in the way people express emotions. The sentiment is opinion-based, not fact-based. This study aims at identifying negative expressions in calls, especially angry customers who are not satisfied with the services, or the business rules, or the systems of rules. By identifying and studying these types of cases, the business can improve call center services and fix the possible business or system issues.

Guidelines are set up for the annotation. The customer negative tag is for negative emotions (e.g. "I hate the system"), attitudes (e.g. "I am not following you"), evaluations (e.g. "your service is the worst"), and negative facts caused by other parties (e.g. "I never received my card"). Other negative facts are not considered as negative (e.g. "My wife died, I need to remove her from my dependents"). The guidelines for CSRs are different. Well trained CSRs usually do not respond negatively, but there are cases that they cannot help the customers. We identify these cases as negative. Cases where a CSR cannot help the customer usually involve business process or system issues.

The sentiment is not always explicit in the text. Borderline linguistic utterances stated loudly and quickly are usually identified as negative (e.g. the utterance "Trust me, it could be done" is classified as negative, since it is in the context that the representative fails to help the customer to enroll in the health plan, and in the audio, the customer is irritated). In all the multimodal sentiment analysis, the labels of all modalities are kept consistent for the same utterance. In our data annotation process, we also keep both text and audio labels that agree with each other and the annotation is based on the audio segments.

3.4 Semi-supervised Learning Annotation Pipeline

To successfully run and train analytical models, massive quantities of stored data are needed. Creating large annotated datasets can be a very time consuming and labor-intensive process. To keep

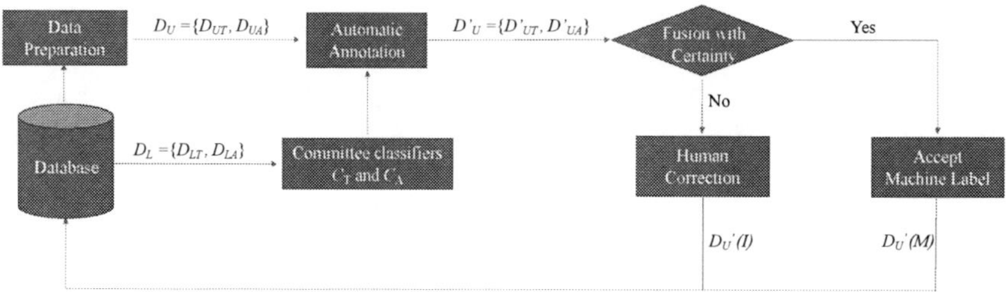

Figure 2: Semi-supervised learning annotation pipeline

the human annotation effort to a minimum, a semi-supervised learning annotation scheme is applied to tag the polarity of utterances as negative, or non-negative. Figure 2 illustrates the process which is similar to active learning annotation. It takes as input a set of labeled examples D_L including text D_{LT} and audio D_{LA}, as well as a larger set of unlabeled examples $D_U = \{D_{UT}, D_{UA}\}$, and produces committee classifiers $C = \{C_T, C_A\}$ and a relatively small set of newly labeled data $D'_U(I)$ and $D'_U(M)$ (Olsson, 2008).

Semi-supervised learning annotation cooperates with humans and machines and combines both semi-supervised learning and multiple classifiers approach for corpus annotation. This pipeline consists of several steps: data generation to obtain D_U (Section 3.2), model training for both modalities to obtain C_T and C_A using D_{LT} and D_{LA} (Section 4), model deployment to get machine label $D'_U = \{D'_{UT}, D'_{UA}\}$, model fusion (Section 5) and results evaluation to decide whether to accept machine label $D'_U(M)$ or ask a human annotator for classifications of the utterances to obtain $D'_U(I)$, then move $D'_U(I)$ and $D'_U(M)$ from D'_U to D_L. It is cyclical and iterative as every step is repeated to continuously improve the accuracy of the classifier and achieve a successful algorithm.

Note, the classifiers in committee $C = \{C_T, C_A\}$ are modified based on D_L in each iteration. The annotation process starts with 20 calls selected from the service center by human domain experts, 20 calls are chunked to 1410 segments via data preparation processing and annotated by three annotators manually as D_L. For the first three iterations, set $C_T=\{$Support Vector Machine (SVM), VADER, AWSSA*, AWSCC†, GoogleSA‡$\}$ requires a small size of training data or no extra training data. As the size of D_{LT} increases, we form a new com-

mittee $C_T = \{$SVM, Long Short-Term Memory (LSTM), Bidirectional Long Short-Term Memory (BLSTM)$\}$. These classifiers are described in Section 4.1. Section 4.2 introduced $C_A = \{$Elastic-Net Regularized Generalized Linear Models (Elastic-Net), K-Nearest Neighbors (KNN), Random Forest (RF), Gaussian Mixture Model (unsupervised GMM) $\}$. In the later iterations, Recurrent Neural Networks (RNN) such as LSTM and BLSTM are applied.

If one call has a long duration ($T > 10$ minutes) and a high percentage of negative utterances based on D'_U ($> 40\%$ for customer or $> 20\%$ for CSR), then we say this call is potentially negative and informative. We then ask an annotator to manually correct the annotated tags D'_U by listening to the call, and move the results $D'_U(I)$ to D_L. For all the other calls, we only keep the utterances where classifiers all agree as $D'_U(M)$. We then remove chunks that are too short (duration $< 1s$) or too long (duration $>20s$). Finally, we discard chunks where the annotator cannot discern classification.

Using the pipeline, 6,565 negative and 10,322 non-negative call clips are annotated as the training dataset. The training data D_{LT} still include transcription errors, even though the threshold discussed in the above paragraph is set to eliminate these utterances to add to the training dataset. In addition, 18,705 cleaned text chat data collected from chat windows are also added to D_{LT} via the annotation pipeline to improve the C_T accuracy. Instead of checking fusion with certainty, we only keep the utterances with classifiers in C_T all agree as $D'_U(M) = D'_{UT}(M)$.

Because of the quality of the calls, the poor performance of the ASR for some cases, and the threshold used to annotate the utterances, more than half of the original call segments are discarded*, and 18,705 text chat data are added to

---

*AWS Comprehend Sentiment Analysis API
†AWS Custom Classification API
‡Google Language Sentiment Analysis API

*The accuracy on the test data decreases by 8% when including all the call segments in the training dataset.

D_{LT}={transcription data, *chat data*} without the corresponding audio files in D_{LA}. It is hard to consider the context of the conversation since the segments are not continuing in the training dataset. Therefore, conversation models are not considered in our committee classifiers C.

4   Bimodal Sentiment Analysis

To model information for sentiment analysis from calls, we first obtain the streams corresponding to each modality via the methods described in Section 3.2, followed by the extraction of a representative set of features for each modality. These features are then used as cues to build classifiers of binary sentiment.

4.1   Sentiment Analysis of Textual Data

General approaches such as sentiment lexicons and sentiment APIs are easy to apply. Both approaches are employed in C_T to monitor the utterance prediction labels in the early stage of semi-supervised learning annotation to extend training data.

VADER (Hutto and Gilbert, 2015) is a simple rule-based model for general sentiment analysis. The results have four categories: compound, negative, neutral, and positive. We classify utterances with negative output as negative, neutral and positive as nonnegative[†] so that it is consistent with BSCD annotation. This model has many advantages, such as being less computationally expensive and easily interpretable. However, one of the main issues with only using lexicons is that most utterances do not contain polarized words. The utterances without polarized words are usually classified as neutral or nonnegative[‡].

Sentiment analysis API is another way to classify sentiment without extra training data. Amazon offers Sentiment Analysis in Amazon Comprehend (AWSSA), which uses machine learning to find insights and relationships in a text. The result returns Mixed, Negative, Neutral, or Positive classification. To be consistent with the BSCD we created, Neutral and Positive are combined as one class: nonnegative[†]. Another sentiment analysis on Google Cloud Natural Language API (GoogleSA) also performs sentiment analysis on text. Sentiment analysis attempts to determine the overall attitude

and is represented by numerical scores and magnitude values. We simply set utterances with negative scores as negative and nonnegative otherwise.

For machine learning-oriented techniques by linguistic features, we evaluated well-known SVM, LSTM, and BLSTM models. Since the data is unbalanced and we want the model to focus more on the negative class, we apply weighted loss functions during the training. Hyperparameters are tuned for each model, and ensemble models are also developed by taking the weighted majority vote.

4.2   Sentiment Analysis of Acoustic Data

Feature engineering heavily relies on expert knowledge about data features. To better understand the human hearing process, we study the acoustic features based on human perception. Three perceptual categories are described in this section. Their corresponding features are usually short-term based features that are extracted from every short-term window (or frame). Long-term features can be generated by aggregating the short-term features extracted from several consecutive frames within a time window. For each short-term acoustic feature, we calculated nine statistical aggregations: mean, standard deviation, quantiles (5%, 25%, 50%, 75%, 95%), range (95%-5% quantile), and interquartile range (75%-25% quantile) to get the long-term features of each segment.

- **Loudness** is the subjective perception of sound pressure which is related to sound intensity. Amplitude and mean frequency spectrum features are extracted to measure loudness. The greater the amplitude of the vibrations, the greater the amount of energy carried by the wave, and the more intense the sound will be.

- **Sharpness** is a measure of the high-frequency content of a sound, the greater the proportion of high frequencies the sharper the sound. Fundamental frequency (pitch) and dominant frequency are extracted.

- **Speaking rate** is normally defined as the number of words spoken per minute. In general, the speaking rate is characterized by different parameters of speech such as pause and vowel durations. In our study, speaking rate is measured by pause duration, character per second (CPS), and word per second (WPS) which are calculated as following

---

[†] Utterances with compound or mixed class are very few, and they are discarded to keep the training data clear.

[‡] This conclusion is verified by the high Rec(+) and low Rec(-) shown in table 1.

for the ith segment:

$$\text{Pause duration}_i = \frac{T_i^{silence}}{T_i^{total}}$$

$$\text{CPS}_i = \frac{N_i^{character}}{T_i^{total}}, \qquad \text{WPS}_i = \frac{N_i^{word}}{T_i^{total}}$$

where for segment i, T_i denotes the time, and N_i denotes the number of characters or words in the corresponding transcription. Pause duration can be interpreted as the percentage of the time where the speaker is silent in each segment. The three variables are aggregated statistics, long-term features.

In nonnegative cases, speakers are in a relaxed and normal emotional state. An agitated or angry emotional state speaker is typically characterized by increased vocal loudness, sharpness, and speaking rate. C_A ={Elastic-Net, KNN, RF, GMM} are built based on the 39 selected features.

Hand-crafted features are generally very successful for specificity sound analysis tasks. One of the main drawbacks of feature engineering is that it relies on transformations that are defined beforehand and ignore some particularities of the signals observed at runtime such as recording conditions and recording devices. A more common approach is to select and adapt features initially introduced for other tasks. A now well-established example of this trend is the popularity of MFCC features (Serizel et al., 2018). In our experiments, MFCC is extracted from each segment and fed to RNN models in later iterations with $|D_{LA}| > 10,000$.

5 Fusion

There are two main fusion techniques: feature-level fusion and decision-level fusion. In our experiments, we employ decision-level fusion. Decision-level fusion has many advantages (Poria et al., 2015). One benefit of the decision-level fusion is we can use classifiers for text and audio features separately. The unimodal classifier can use data from another communication channel of the same type to improve its accuracy, e.g. text data from the chat windows is borrowed to improve the C_T accuracy in our study. Separating modalities permit us to use any learner suitable for the particular problem at hand. In practice, the two unimodal classifiers can be applied separately, e.g. to analyze text data from chat windows $D_U = D_{UT}$, apply C_T only to get sentiment labels D'_{UT}, then add $D'_{UT}(M)$ to D_{LT}. Another benefit of the decision-level fusion is its processing speed since fewer features are used for each classifier and separate classifiers can be run in parallel.

Decision-level fusion usually adds probabilities or summarized predictions from each unimodal classifier with weights or takes the majority voting among the predicted class labels by unimodal classifiers.

In this paper, various fusion methods are evaluated, including two novel approaches that use linguistic ensemble results as the baseline, while then checking acoustic results to modify classification decisions. In Fus1, if the audio ensemble classifies negative and one or more text models classifies negative, we then reclassify the result to negative. In Fus2, if the audio ensemble classifies a sample as negative, we then reclassify the result to negative directly without checking the linguistic modality. The Fus1 and Fus2 approaches are proposed, because for borderline linguistic utterances, acoustic features are more important than linguistic features to understand the spoken intention of the speaker.

6 Experiment Results

The test dataset consists of 21 calls with 1,890 utterances, which are manually annotated for negative (848) and nonnegative (1,042).

6.1 Evaluation Measures

As evaluation measures, we rely on accuracy and weighted F1-score, which is the weighted harmonic mean of precision and recall. Precision is the probability of returning values that are correct. Recall, also known as sensitivity is the probability of relevant values that the algorithm outputs.

As shown in Table 1, general approaches in C_T, Vader and APIs, tend to have a low negative recall. The semantic knowledge based classifiers have more than 20% higher weighted F1-score than the general approaches. The classifiers are trained on D_{LT}={transcription data, chat data}. The overall weighted F1-score is more than 10% higher than the classifiers trained on call transcription only data[§].

BLSTM on MFCC performs better than $C_A =$ {Elastic-Net (penalty $0.2||\beta||_1 + 0.4||\beta||_2^2$), KNN ($k = 3$), RF, GMM} on acoustic features. Using audio features alone, a weighted F1-score of 0.584

[§]Weighted F1-scores are 0.718 (SVM), 0.719 (LSTM) and 0.714 (BLSTM).

Methods	Text						Audio				
	SVM	LSTM	BLSTM	Vader	AWSSA	GoogleSA	Elastic-Net	KNN	RF	GMM	BLSTM
Acc.	0.814	0.853	0.843	0.498	0.651	0.637	0.570	0.544	0.585	0.546	0.601
F1 (w)	0.814	0.852	0.842	0.347	0.628	0.615	0.500	0.534	0.549	0.500	0.584
Prec.(+)	0.770	0.802	0.781	0.494	0.594	0.586	0.528	0.518	0.541	0.513	0.561
Prec.(-)	0.871	0.92	0.934	0.742	0.821	0.779	0.860	0.589	0.741	0.685	0.693
Rec. (+)	0.886	0.929	0.946	0.991	0.908	0.881	0.964	0.697	0.883	0.872	0.811
Rec. (-)	0.746	0.779	0.745	0.024	0.404	0.402	0.205	0.402	0.309	0.252	0.402

Table 1: Binary classification of sentiment polarity on test data: Accuracy (Acc.), weighted F1-score (F1 (w)), precision (Prec.) and recall (Rec.) for the nonnegative (+) and negative (-) classes

Methods	Ensemble			Fusion	
	Text	Audio	T+A	Fus1	Fus2
Acc.	0.851	0.586	0.846	0.858	0.871
F1 (w)	0.851	0.525	0.846	0.858	0.871
Prec.(+)	0.779	0.531	0.800	0.790	0.818
Prec.(-)	0.949	0.927	0.896	0.946	0.933
Rec. (+)	0.953	0.979	0.894	0.950	0.933
Rec. (-)	0.761	0.240	0.804	0.777	0.817

Table 2: Binary classification of sentiment polarity on both linguistic and acoustic modalities

can be reached, which is acceptable considering that the real world audio-only system exclusively analyzes the tone of the speaker's voice and doesn't consider any language information.

The acoustic modality is significantly weaker than the linguistic modality. Usually, speakers' tones are not signifcantly different from the tones under normal emotional state even the content is negative (e.g. "We messed up." with negative tag). 97% of the segments with correct D'_{UT} but wrong D'_{UA} have negative as true tag. The other 3% are the nonnegate segments with emphasized words (e.g. " But I do have a newborn coming." with nonnegtive tag).

In most cases, text already includes enough information to judge the sentiment. A few observed typical situations leading to linguistic modality misclassification are the presence of misleading linguistic cues caused by overlapping or other issues (e.g. ASR "Customer: I love it. It can be done." and true transcription "CSR: I... Customer: Drop it. It can be done." with negative tag), ambiguous linguistic utterances whose sentiment polarity are highly dependent on the context described in earlier or later part of the call (e.g. "But I got a call from your service center today apologizing, saying, Yeah, we made a mistake." with nonnegative tag), or nonnegative linguistic utterances stated angrily (e.g. "So I think you should honor those amounts." with negative tag).

In order to achieve better accuracy, we combine the two modalities together to exploit complementary information. We simply combine results of the three semantic knowledge based classifiers and all the five audio classifiers by taking the weighted majority vote. The T+A ensemble results are shown in Table 2 and they do not improve when compared to the unimodal text ensemble results.

Since the unimodal performance of linguistic modality is notably better than acoustic modality, our decision-level fusion methods use linguistic ensemble results as the base-line, while acoustic results are used as supplemental information to calibrate each classification. Fus1 reclassifies the ambiguous linguistic utterances, and Fus2 reclassifies the nonnegative/ambiguous linguistic utterances based on audio ensemble classifies. The two novel fusion approaches discussed in Section 5 are tested. The Fus2 bimodal system yields a 2% improvement in weighted F1-score than the text unimodal system.

McNemar's test is applied to compare the accuracy of text only results D'_{UT} and Fus2 results D'_{UF2}

$$\chi^2 = \frac{(14 - 52)^2}{14 + 52} = 21.88,$$

where the number of segments with correct D'_{UT} wrong D'_{UF2} is 14, and wrong D'_{UT} correct D'_{UF2} is 52. The McNemar's test gives $\chi^2 = 21.88$ and $P < 0.001$, which implies a statistically significant effect by adding acoustic features using the Fus2 approach.

The acoustic modality provides important cues to identify borderline linguistic segments with negative emotions. Our results show that relying on the joint use of linguistic and acoustic modalities allows us to better sense the sentiment being expressed as compared to the use of only one modality at a time. The acoustic feature analysis helps us to better understand the spoken intention of the

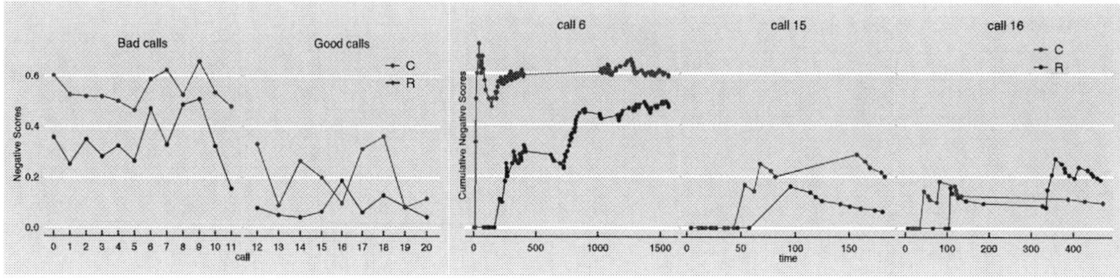

Figure 3: The (cumulative) negative score pattern between customers (C) and CSRs (R)

speaker, which is not normally expressed through text.

6.2 Tempo Sentiment Pattern

The sentiment is not only regarded as an internal psychological phenomena but also interpreted and processed communicatively through social interactions. Conversations exemplify such a scenario where inter-personal sentiment influences persist.

The left panel in Figure 3 shows the negative scores of customers and CSRs in 21 test calls. The negative score, a weighted negative segment percentage, is calculated to analyze the overall sentiment. Weights 0.8, 1, and 1.2 are assigned to the first third, second third and last third of each call. Since long pauses in calls are discarded in the data preparation process, these segments do not have sentiment labels and do not contribute to the negative score. The negative scores of CRSs are commonly lower than customers', and usually high negative scores for customers correspond to high negative scores for CSRs. We can conclude from the figure that sentiment can be affected by other parties during a conversation.

To further analyze the interactions between customers and CSRs, the cumulative negative scores for call 6, 15, and 16 are drawn on the right panel of Figure 3. The x-axis shows time of the whole call in seconds including noise and long pauses. Call 6 shows the sentiment patterns of a typical bad call, which is characterized by long duration and long pauses. The two long pauses are from 444s to 607s and from 921s to 1008s. Between the two long pauses, there are three customer and CSR overlapping segments, but the Automatic Speaker Diarization recognizes all of them as CSRs. The customer has a high negative score from beginning to end, and the CSR fails to help the customer during the call. Call 15 is a typical good call. The overall negative score is low and the negative score

pattern goes down for both the customer and the CSR, which means the problem is resolved by the end of the call. Call 16 is another type of call, in which the customer does not get angry even though the CSR is unable to solve his/her issues.

7 Discussion and Future Work

A new dataset BSCD consisting of real-world conversation, the service calls, is introduced. Human communication is a dynamic process, and our eventual goal is to develop a bimodal sentiment analysis engine with the ability to learn the temporal interaction sentiment patterns among conversation parties. In the process of fusion, we have approached the study of audio sentiment analysis from an angle that is somewhat different from most people's.
Future research will concentrate on evaluations using larger data sets, exploring more acoustic feature relevance analysis, and striving to improve the decision-level fusion process.
A call is constituent of a group of utterances that have contextual dependencies among them. However, in our semi-supervised learning annotation pipeline, about half of the segments in calls are discarded. Therefore the interdependent modeling is out of the scope of this paper and we include it as future work.

Acknowledgements

The author wishes to express sincere appreciation to Sony SungChu for the support of the project and the comments that greatly improved the manuscript, and the anonymous reviewers for their insightful suggestions to help clarify the manuscript.

References

Gustavo Aguilar, Viktor Rozgic, Weiran Wang, and Chao Wang. 2019. Multimodal and multi-view models for emotion recognition. arXiv:1906.10198. Version 1.

Samah Alhazmi, Bill Black, and J McNaught. 2013. Arabic SentiWordNet in relation to SentiWordNet 3.0. *International Journal of Computational Linguistics*, 4:1–11.

Carlos Busso, Murtaza Bulut, Chi-Chun Lee, Abe Kazemzadeh, Emily Mower Provost, Samuel Kim, Jeannette Chang, Sungbok Lee, and Shrikanth Narayanan. 2008. IEMOCAP: Interactive emotional dyadic motion capture database. *Language Resources and Evaluation*, 42:335–359.

Erik Cambria, J. Fu, Federica Bisio, and Soujanya Poria. 2015. AffectiveSpace 2: Enabling affective intuition for concept-level sentiment analysis. *Proc. AAAI*, pages 508–514.

Erik Cambria, Devamanyu Hazarika, Soujanya Poria, Amir Hussain, and Rbv Subramanyam. 2017. Benchmarking multimodal sentiment analysis. arXiv:1707.09538. Version 1.

Erik Cambria, Robyn Speer, C. Havasi, and Amir Hussain. 2010. SenticNet: A publicly available semantic resource for opinion mining. *AAAI Fall Symposium - Technical Report*, pages 14–18.

Jean Carletta, Simone Ashby, Sebastien Bourban, Mike Flynn, Mael Guillemot, Thomas Hain, Jaroslav Kadlec, Vasilis Karaiskos, Wessel Kraaij, Melissa Kronenthal, Guillaume Lathoud, Mike Lincoln, Agnes Lisowska, Iain McCowan, Wilfried Post, Dennis Reidsma, and Pierre Wellner. 2006. The AMI meeting corpus: A pre-announcement. In *Proceedings of the Second International Conference on Machine Learning for Multimodal Interaction*, pages 28–39, Berlin, Heidelberg. Springer-Verlag.

Florian Eyben, Martin Wöllmer, and Björn Schuller. 2010. openSMILE – the munich versatile and fast open-source audio feature extractor. *MM'10 - Proceedings of the ACM Multimedia 2010 International Conference*, pages 1459–1462.

Florian Eyben, Martin Wllmer, and Björn Schuller. 2009. openEAR - introducing the munich open-source emotion and affect recognition toolkit. *Affective Computing and Intelligent Interaction and Workshops, 2009. ACII 2009. 3rd International Conference*, pages 1 – 6.

Alec Go, Richa Bhayani, and Lei Huang. 2009. Twitter sentiment classification using distant supervision. *CS224N Project Report*, 150.

Devamanyu Hazarika, Soujanya Poria, Rada Mihalcea, Erik Cambria, and Roger Zimmermann. 2018. ICON: Interactive conversational memory network for multimodal emotion detection. pages 2594–2604.

C.J. Hutto and Eric Gilbert. 2015. VADER: A parsimonious rule-based model for sentiment analysis of social media text. *Proceedings of the 8th International Conference on Weblogs and Social Media, ICWSM 2014*.

Manas Jain, Shruthi Narayan, Pratibha Balaji, Abhijit Bhowmick, and Rajesh Muthu. 2018. Speech emotion recognition using support vector machine.

Margarita Kotti and Fabio Paternò. 2012. Speaker-independent emotion recognition exploiting a psychologically-inspired binary cascade classification schema. *Int J Speech Technol*, 15.

Bing Liu. 2010. Sentiment analysis and subjectivity. *Handbook of Natural Language Processing, Second Edition*.

Bing Liu. 2012. Sentiment analysis and opinion mining. In *Synthesis Lectures on Human Language Technologies*.

Navonil Majumder, Soujanya Poria, Devamanyu Hazarika, Rada Mihalcea, Alexander Gelbukh, and Erik Cambria. 2019. DialogueRNN: An attentive RNN for emotion detection in conversations. *Proceedings of the AAAI Conference on Artificial Intelligence*, 33:6818–6825.

Daniel McEnnis, Cory McKay, Ichiro Fujinaga, and Philippe Depalle. 2005. jAudio: An feature extraction library. *Proceedings of the International Conference on Music Information Retrieval*, pages 600–603.

Brian McFee, Colin Raffel, Dawen Liang, Daniel Ellis, Matt Mcvicar, Eric Battenberg, and Oriol Nieto. 2015. librosa: Audio and music signal analysis in python. *in Proceedings of the 14th Python in Science Conference*, 8:18–24.

Gary Mckeown, Michel Valstar, Roddy Cowie, and Maja Pantic. 2010. The SEMAINE corpus of emotionally coloured character interactions. *2010 IEEE International Conference on Multimedia and Expo, ICME 2010*, pages 1079–1084.

Gary Mckeown, Michel Valstar, Roddy Cowie, Maja Pantic, and M. Schroder. 2013. The SEMAINE database: Annotated multimodal records of emotionally colored conversations between a person and a limited agent. *Affective Computing, IEEE Transactions on*, 3:5–17.

Finn Nielsen. 2011. A new ANEW: Evaluation of a word list for sentiment analysis in microblogs. *CoRR*.

Fredrik Olsson. 2008. Bootstrapping named entity annotation by means of active machine learning: a method for creating corpora.

Y Pan, P Shen, and L Shen. 2012. Speech emotion recognition using support vector machine. *Int. J. Smart Home*, 6:101–108.

Bo Pang and Lillian Lee. 2004a. A sentimental education: Sentiment analysis using subjectivity summarization based on minimum cuts. *Computing Research Repository - CORR*, 271-278:271–278.

Bo Pang and Lillian Lee. 2004b. A sentimental education: Sentiment analysis using subjectivity summarization based on minimum cuts. In *Proceedings of the 42nd Annual Meeting of the Association for Computational Linguistics (ACL-04)*, pages 271–278, Barcelona, Spain.

James Pennebaker, Cindy Chung, Molly Ireland, Amy Gonzales, and Roger Booth. 2007. The development and psychometric properties of LIWC2007.

James Pennebaker, M. Francis, and R. Booth. 2001. Linguistic inquiry and word count (LIWC): LIWC2001. 71.

Soujanya Poria. 2016. Fusing audio, visual and textual clues for sentiment analysis from multimodal content. *Neurocomputing*, 174:50–59.

Soujanya Poria, Erik Cambria, and Alexander Gelbukh. 2015. Deep convolutional neural network textual features and multiple kernel learning for utterance-level multimodal sentiment analysis. In *Proceedings of the 2015 Conference on Empirical Methods in Natural Language Processing*, pages 2539–2544, Lisbon, Portugal. Association for Computational Linguistics.

Soujanya Poria, Erik Cambria, Amir Hussain, and Guang-Bin Huang. 2014a. Towards an intelligent framework for multimodal affective data analysis. *Neural Networks*, 63.

Soujanya Poria, Alexander Gelbukh, Erik Cambria, Amir Hussain, and Guang-Bin Huang. 2014b. EmoSenticSpace: A novel framework for affective common-sense reasoning. *Knowledge-Based Systems*, 69.

Soujanya Poria, Navonil Majumder, Rada Mihalcea, and Eduard Hovy. 2019. Emotion recognition in conversation: Research challenges, datasets, and recent advances. arXiv:1905.02947. Version 1.

Cícero dos Santos and Maíra Gatti. 2014. Deep convolutional neural networks for sentiment analysis of short texts. In *Proceedings of COLING 2014, the 25th International Conference on Computational Linguistics: Technical Papers*, pages 69–78, Dublin, Ireland. Dublin City University and Association for Computational Linguistics.

Björn Schuller, Michel Valstar, Roddy Cowie, and Maja Pantic. 2012. AVEC 2012 – the continuous audio/visual emotion challenge. *ICMI'12 - Proceedings of the ACM International Conference on Multimodal Interaction.*

Romain Serizel, Victor Bisot, Slim Essid, and Gaël Richard. 2018. Acoustic features for environmental sound analysis. *Computational Analysis of Sound Scenes and Events*, pages 71–101.

Caifeng Shan, Shaogang Gong, and Peter W. Mcowan. 2007. Beyond facial expressions: Learning human emotion from body gestures. In *in Proc. British Machine Vision Conf.*

Richard Socher, Alex Perelygin, Jean Y. Wu, Jason Chuang, Christopher D. Manning, Andrew .Y. Ng, and Christopher Potts. 2013. Recursive deep models for semantic compositionality over a sentiment treebank. *EMNLP*, 1631:1631–1642.

Philip Stone, Dexter Dunphy, Marshall Smith, and Daniel Ogilvie. 1966. *The General Inquirer: A Computer Approach to Content Analysis*, volume 4.

Carlo Strapparava and Rada Mihalcea. 2007. SemEval-2007 task 14: Affective text. *Proceedings of the 4th International Workshop on the Semantic Evaluations (SemEval 2007).*

Jerome Sueur, Thierry Aubin, and Caroline Simonis. 2008. Seewave: a free modular tool for sound analysis and synthesis. *Bioacoustics*, 18:213–226.

Yequan Wang, Minlie Huang, Xiaoyan Zhu, and Li Zhao. 2016. Attention-based LSTM for aspect-level sentiment classification. In *Proceedings of the 2016 Conference on Empirical Methods in Natural Language Processing*, pages 606–615, Austin, Texas. Association for Computational Linguistics.

Janyce Wiebe, Theresa Wilson, and Claire Cardie. 2005. Annotating expressions of opinions and emotions in language. *Language Resources and Evaluation (formerly Computers and the Humanities)*, 39:164–210.

Theresa Wilson, Janyce Wiebe, and Paul Hoffmann. 2005. Recognizing contextual polarity in phrase-level sentiment analysis. *Proceedings of HLT/EMNLP.*

Z. Zeng, J. Tu, M. Liu, T. S. Huang, B. Pianfetti, D. Roth, and S. Levinson. 2007. Audio-visual affect recognition. *IEEE Transactions on Multimedia*, 9(2):424–428.

Using Large Pretrained Language Models for Answering User Queries from Product Specifications

Kalyani Roy[1], Smit Shah[1]*, Nithish Pai[2], Jaidam Ramtej[2], Prajit Prashant Nadkarn[2], Jyotirmoy Banerjee[2], Pawan Goyal[1], and Surender Kumar[2]

[1]Indian Institute of Technology Kharagpur

[2]Flipkart

kroy@iitkgp.ac.in, smitsunny11@gmail.com, {nithish.p, jaidam.ramtej, prajit.pn }@ flipkart.com, jyoban@gmail.com, pawang@cse.iitkgp.ac.in, surender.k@flipkart.com

Abstract

While buying a product from the e-commerce websites, customers generally have a plethora of questions. From the perspective of both the e-commerce service provider as well as the customers, there must be an effective question answering system to provide immediate answers to the user queries. While certain questions can only be answered after using the product, there are many questions which can be answered from the product specification itself. Our work takes a first step in this direction by finding out the relevant product specifications, that can help answering the user questions. We propose an approach to automatically create a training dataset for this problem. We utilize recently proposed XLNet and BERT architectures for this problem and find that they provide much better performance than the Siamese model, previously applied for this problem (Lai et al., 2018). Our model gives a good performance even when trained on one vertical and tested across different verticals.

1 Introduction

Product specifications are the attributes of a product. These specifications help a user to easily identify and differentiate products and choose the one that matches certain specifications. There are more than 80 million products across $80+$ product categories on Flipkart [1]. The 6 largest categories are - *Mobile, AC, Backpack, Computer, Shoes,* and *Watches*. A large fraction of user queries ($\sim 20\%$)[2] can be answered with the specifications. Product specifications would be helpful in providing instant responses to questions newly posed by users about

---

* Work done while author was at IIT Kharagpur.

[1]Flipkart Pvt Ltd. is an e-commerce company based in Bangalore, India.

[2]We randomly sampled 1500 questions from all these verticals except *Mobile* and manually annotated them as to whether these can be answered through product specifications.

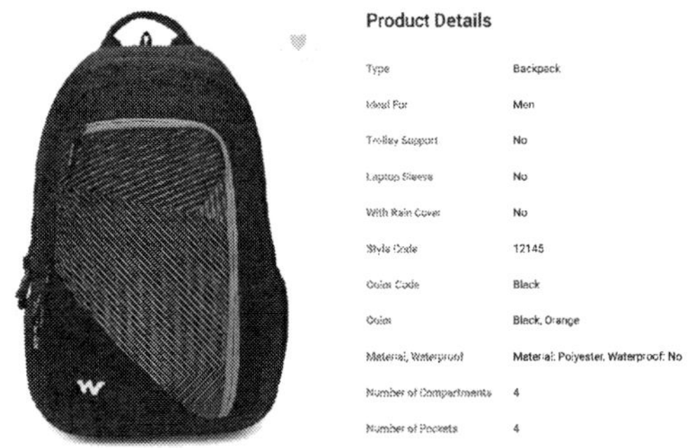

Figure 1: Snapshot of a product with its specifications.

the corresponding product. Consider a question "What is the fabric of this bag?" This new question can be easily answered by retrieving the specification "Material" as the response. Fig. 1 depicts this scenario.

Most of the recent works on product related queries on e-commerce leverage the product reviews to answer the questions (Gao et al., 2019; Zhao et al., 2019; McAuley and Yang, 2016). Although reviews are a rich source of data, they are also subject to personal experiences. People tend to give many reviews on some products and since it is based upon their personal experience, the opinion is also diverse. This creates a massive volume and range of opinions and thus makes review systems difficult to navigate. Sometimes products do not even have any reviews that can be used to find an answer, also the reviews do not mention the specifications a lot, but mainly deal with the experience. So, there are several reasons why product specifications might be a useful source of information to answer product-related queries which does not involve user experience to find an answer. As the specifications are readily available, users can get the response instantly.

Proceedings of the 3rd Workshop on e-Commerce and NLP (ECNLP 3), pages 35–39
Online, July 10, 2020. ©2020 Association for Computational Linguistics

Dataset	Products	Questions	Avg. Specs
Mobile	1,175	260,529	55
AC	300	16,545	35
Backpack	300	16,878	17
Computer	300	93,589	60
Shoes	300	5,812	10
Watches	300	21,392	50

Table 1: Statistics of 6 largest categories.

This paper attempts to retrieve the product specifications that would answer the user queries. While solving this problem, our key contributions are as follows - (i) We demonstrate the success of XLNet on finding product specifications that can help answering product related queries. It beats the baseline Siamese method by $0.14 - 0.31$ points in HIT@1. (ii) We utilize a method to automatically create a large training dataset using a semi-supervised approach, that was used to fine-tune XLNet and other models. (iii) While we trained on *Mobile* vertical, we tested on different verticals, namely, *AC*, *Backpack*, *Computer*, *Shoes*, *Watches*, which show promising results.

2 Background and Related Work

In recent years, e-commerce product question answering (PQA) has received a lot of attention. Yu et al. (2018) present a framework to answer product related questions by retrieving a ranked list of reviews and they employ the Positional Language Model (PLM) to create the training data. Chen et al. (2019) apply a multi-task attentive model to identify plausible answers. Lai et al. (2018) propose a Siamese deep learning model for answering questions regarding product specifications. The model returns a score for a question and specification pair. McAuley and Yang (2016) exploit product reviews for answer prediction via a Mixture of Expert (MoE) model. This MoE model makes use of a review relevance function and an answer prediction function. It assumes that a candidate answer set containing the correct answers is available for answer selection. Cui et al. (2017) develop a chatbot for e-commerce sites known as SuperAgent. SuperAgent considers question answer collections, reviews and specifications when answering questions. It selects the best answer from multiple data sources. Language representation models like BERT (Devlin et al., 2019) and XLNet (Yang et al., 2019) are pre-trained on vast amounts of text and then fine-tuned on task-specific labelled data. The resulting models have achieved state of the art in many natural language processing tasks including question answering. Dzendzik et al. (2019) employ BERT to answer binary questions by utilizing customer reviews.

In this paper, unlike some of the previous works (Lai et al., 2018; Chen et al., 2019) on PQA that solely rely on human annotators to annotate the training instances, we propose a semi-supervised method to label training data. We leverage the product specifications to answer user queries by using BERT and XLNet.

3 Problem Statement

Here, we formalize the problem of answering user queries from product specifications. Given a question Q about a product P and the list of M specifications $\{s_1, s_2, ..., s_M\}$ of P, our objective is to identify the specification s_i that can help answer Q. Here, we assume that the question is answerable from specifications.

4 Model Architecture

Our goal is to train a classifier that takes a question and a specification as input (e.g., "Color Code Black") and predicts whether the specification is relevant to the question. We take Siamese architecture (Lai et al., 2018) as our baseline method. We fine-tune BERT and XLNet for this classification task.

Siamese: We train a 100-dimensional word2vec embedding on the whole corpus (all questions and specifications as shown in Table 1.) to get the input word representation. In the Siamese model, the question and specification is passed through a Siamese Bi-LSTM layer. Then we use max-pooling on the contextual representations to get the feature vectors of the question and specification. We concatenate the absolute difference and hadamard product of these two feature vectors and feed it to two fully connected layers of dimension 50 and 25, subsequently. Finally, the softmax layer gives the relevance score.

BERT and **XLNet :** The architecture we use for fine-tuning BERT and XLNet is the same. We begin with the pre-trained BERT$_{\text{Base}}$ and XLNet$_{\text{Base}}$ model. To adapt the models for our task, we introduce a fully-connected layer over the final hidden state corresponding to the [CLS] input token. During fine-tuning, we optimize the entire model end-to-end, with the additional softmax classifier parameters $W \in R^{K \times H}$, where H is the dimen-

Dataset	# que-spec pairs	Answer type (in %)		
		Num	Y/N	Other
AC	3693	0.27	0.52	0.21
Backpack	2693	0.29	0.48	0.23
Computer	2718	0.04	0.78	0.18
Shoes	999	0.09	0.49	0.42
Watches	1700	0.17	0.59	0.24

Table 2: Test datasets statistics.

sion of the hidden state vectors and K is the number of classes.

5 Experimental Setup

5.1 Dataset Creation

The Statistics for the 6 largest categories used in this paper are shown in Table 1, containing a snapshot of product details up to January 2019. Except for mobiles, for other domains, 300 products were sampled. As the number of question-specification pairs is huge, manually labelling a sufficiently large dataset is a tedious task. So, we propose a semi-supervised method to create a large training dataset using Dual Embedding Space model (DESM) (Mitra et al., 2016).

Suppose a product P has S specifications and Q questions. For a question $q_i \in Q$ and a specification $s_j \in S$, we find dual embedding score $DUAL(q_i, s_j)$ using Equation 1, where t_q and t_s denote the vectors for the question and specification terms, respectively. We consider (q_i, s_j) pair positive if $DUAL(q_i, s_j) \geq \theta$ and negative if $DUAL(q_i, s_j) < \theta$.

$$DUAL(q_i, s_j) = \frac{1}{|q_i|} \sum_{t_q \in q_i} \frac{t_q^T \overline{s_j}}{\| t_q \| \| \overline{s_j} \|} \quad (1)$$

where

$$\overline{s_j} = \frac{1}{|s_j|} \sum_{t_s \in s_j} \frac{t_s}{\| t_s \|} \quad (2)$$

We take $Mobile$ dataset to create labelled training data since most of the questions come from this vertical. We choose the threshold value (θ) which gives the best accuracy on manually labelled balanced validation dataset consisting of 380 question and specification pairs. We train a word2vec (Mikolov et al., 2013) model on our training dataset to get the embeddings of the words. The word2vec model learns two weight matrices during training. The matrix corresponding to the input space and the output space is denoted as IN and OUT word embedding space respectively.

Dataset	Model	HIT@1	HIT@2	HIT@3
AC	BERT-380	0.05	0.09	0.14
	XLNet-380	0.20	0.32	0.39
	Siamese	0.38	0.53	0.61
	BERT	0.62	**0.77**	**0.81**
	XLNet	**0.69**	**0.77**	0.80
Backpack	BERT-380	0.17	0.27	0.34
	XLNet-380	0.27	0.41	0.48
	Siamese	0.35	0.53	0.65
	BERT	**0.50**	0.66	0.69
	XLNet	0.49	**0.67**	**0.70**
Computer	BERT-380	0.14	0.16	0.22
	XLNet-380	0.06	0.16	0.18
	Siamese	0.5	0.6	0.72
	BERT	0.68	0.80	0.90
	XLNet	**0.70**	**0.86**	**0.92**
Shoes	BERT-380	0.22	0.40	0.55
	XLNet-380	0.25	0.45	0.60
	Siamese	0.42	0.55	0.62
	BERT	0.60	0.72	0.84
	XLNet	**0.63**	**0.77**	**0.88**
Watches	BERT-380	0.05	0.09	0.15
	XLNet-380	0.24	0.36	0.45
	Siamese	0.42	0.65	0.69
	BERT	0.54	0.60	0.74
	XLNet	**0.60**	**0.76**	**0.84**

Table 3: Performance comparison of different models.

Word2vec leverages only the input embeddings (IN), but discards the output embeddings (OUT), whereas DESM utilizes both IN and OUT embeddings. To compute the DUAL score of a question and specification, we take OUT-OUT vectors as it gives the best validation accuracy. We find that for $\theta = 0.34$, we gain maximum accuracy value of 0.72 on the validation set. This creates a labelled training dataset $\mathcal{D}$ with $57,138$ positive pairs and $655,290$ negative pairs. For training, we take all the positive data from $\mathcal{D}$ and we randomly sample an equal number of negative examples from $\mathcal{D}$.

To create the test datasets, domain experts manually annotate the correct specification for a question. As the test datasets come from different verticals, there is no product in common with the training set. The details of different test datasets are shown in Table 2. We analyze the questions in the test datasets and find that the questions can be roughly categorized into three classes - numerical, yes/no and others based upon the answer type of the questions. For a question, we have a number of specifications and only one of them is correct.

5.2 Training and Evaluation

We split the $Mobile$ dataset into 80% and 20% as training set and development set, respectively. The Siamese model is trained for 20 epoch with Stochastic Gradient Descent optimizer and learn-

Question	Siamese	BERT	XLNet
Is it single core or multi core?	processor name core i3	internal mic single digital microphone	**number of cores 2**
	processor variant 7100u	processor name core i3	processor name core i3
	os architecture 64 bit	**number of cores 2**	processor brand intel
Does 16 inch laptop fit in to it?	depth 13 inch	**compatible laptop size 15.4 inch**	**compatible laptop size 15.4 inch**
	width 9 inch	laptop sleeve no	depth 13 inch
	height 19 inch	depth 13 inch	height 19 inch

Table 4: Top three specifications returned by different models for two questions. Correct specification is highlighted in bold.

ing rate 0.01. The fine-tuning of BERT and XLNet is done with the same experimental settings as given in the original papers. In all the models, we minimize the cross-entropy loss while training. BERT-380 and XLNet-380 models are fine-tuned on the 380 labeled validation dataset that was used for creating the training dataset in Section 5.1.

During evaluation, we sort the question specification pairs according to their relevance score. From this ranked list, we compute whether the correct specification appears within top $k, k \in \{1, 2, 3\}$ positions. The ratio of correctly identified specifications in top 1, 2, and 3 positions to the total number of questions is denoted as HIT@1, HIT@2 and HIT@3 respectively.

6 Results and Discussion

Table 3 shows the performance of the models on different datasets[3]. BERT-380 and XLNet-380 perform very poorly, but when we use the train dataset created with DESM, there is a large boost in the models' performance and it shows the effectiveness of our semi-supervised method in generating labeled dataset. Both BERT and XLNet outperform the baseline Siamese model (Lai et al., 2018) by a large margin, and retrieve the correct specification within top 3 results for most of the queries. For *Backpack* and *AC*, both BERT and XLNet are very competitive. XLNet outperforms BERT in *Computer*, *Shoes*, and *Watches*. Only in HIT@1 of *AC*, BERT has surpassed XLNet with 0.07 points. We see that all the models have performed better in *Computer* compared to the other datasets. *Computer* has the highest percentage of yes/no questions and this might be one of the reasons, as some questions might have word overlap with correct specification. Table 4 shows the top three specifications returned by different models for some

questions. We see that Siamese architecture returns results which look similar to naïve word match, and retrieve wrong specifications. On the other hand, BERT and XLNet are able to retrieve the correct specifications.

Error Analysis: We assume that for each question, there is only one correct specification, but the correct answer may span multiple specifications and our models can not provide a full answer. For example, in *Backpack* dataset, the dimension of the backpack, i.e., its height, weight, depth is defined separately. So, when user queries about the dimension, only one specification is provided. Some specifications are given in one unit, but users want the answer in another unit, e.g., "what is the width of this bag in cms?". Since the specification is given in inches, the models show the answer in inches. So, the answer is related, but not exactly correct. Users sometimes want to know the difference between certain specification types, what is meant by some specifications. For example, consider the questions "what is the difference between inverter and non-inverter AC?", "what is meant by water resistant depth?". While we can find the type of inverter, the water resistant depth of a watch etc. from specifications, the definition of the specification is not given. As we have generated train data labels in semi-supervised fashion, it also contributes to inaccurate classification in some cases.

7 Conclusion and Future Work

In this paper, we proposed a method to label training data with little supervision. We demonstrated that large pretrained language models such as BERT and XLNet can be fine-tuned successfully to obtain product specifications that can help answer user queries. We also achieve reasonably good results even while testing on different verticals.

We would like to extend our method to take into

---

[3]Unsupervised DUAL embedding model gave very similar results to Siamese model, and is not reported.

account multiple specifications as an answer. We also plan to develop a classifier to identify which questions can not be answered from the specifications.

References

Long Chen, Ziyu Guan, Wei Zhao, Wanqing Zhao, Xiaopeng Wang, Zhou Zhao, and Huan Sun. 2019. Answer identification from product reviews for user questions by multi-task attentive networks. In *Proceedings of the AAAI Conference on Artificial Intelligence*, volume 33, pages 45–52.

Lei Cui, Shaohan Huang, Furu Wei, Chuanqi Tan, Chaoqun Duan, and Ming Zhou. 2017. SuperAgent: A customer service chatbot for e-commerce websites. pages 97–102.

Jacob Devlin, Ming-Wei Chang, Kenton Lee, and Kristina Toutanova. 2019. BERT: Pre-training of deep bidirectional transformers for language understanding. In *Proceedings of the 2019 Conference of the North American Chapter of the Association for Computational Linguistics: Human Language Technologies, Volume 1 (Long and Short Papers)*, pages 4171–4186, Minneapolis, Minnesota. Association for Computational Linguistics.

Daria Dzendzik, Carl Vogel, and Jennifer Foster. 2019. Is it dish washer safe? automatically answering "yes/no" questions using customer reviews. In *Proceedings of the 2019 Conference of the North American Chapter of the Association for Computational Linguistics: Student Research Workshop*, pages 1–6, Minneapolis, Minnesota. Association for Computational Linguistics.

Shen Gao, Zhaochun Ren, Yihong Zhao, Dongyan Zhao, Dawei Yin, and Rui Yan. 2019. Product-aware answer generation in e-commerce question-answering. In *Proceedings of the Twelfth ACM International Conference on Web Search and Data Mining*, WSDM '19, page 429–437, New York, NY, USA. Association for Computing Machinery.

Tuan Lai, Trung Bui, Sheng Li, and Nedim Lipka. 2018. A simple end-to-end question answering model for product information. In *Proceedings of the First Workshop on Economics and Natural Language Processing*, pages 38–43, Melbourne, Australia. Association for Computational Linguistics.

Julian McAuley and Alex Yang. 2016. Addressing complex and subjective product-related queries with customer reviews. In *Proceedings of the 25th International Conference on World Wide Web*, WWW '16, page 625–635, Republic and Canton of Geneva, CHE. International World Wide Web Conferences Steering Committee.

Tomas Mikolov, Ilya Sutskever, Kai Chen, Greg Corrado, and Jeffrey Dean. 2013. Distributed representations of words and phrases and their compositionality. In *Proceedings of the 26th International Conference on Neural Information Processing Systems - Volume 2*, NIPS'13, page 3111–3119, Red Hook, NY, USA. Curran Associates Inc.

Bhaskar Mitra, Eric Nalisnick, Nick Craswell, and Rich Caruana. 2016. A dual embedding space model for document ranking. *arXiv preprint arXiv:1602.01137*.

Zhilin Yang, Zihang Dai, Yiming Yang, Jaime Carbonell, Russ R Salakhutdinov, and Quoc V Le. 2019. Xlnet: Generalized autoregressive pretraining for language understanding. In *Advances in neural information processing systems*, pages 5754–5764.

Qian Yu, Wai Lam, and Zihao Wang. 2018. Responding e-commerce product questions via exploiting QA collections and reviews. In *Proceedings of the 27th International Conference on Computational Linguistics*, pages 2192–2203, Santa Fe, New Mexico, USA. Association for Computational Linguistics.

Jie Zhao, Ziyu Guan, and Huan Sun. 2019. Riker: Mining rich keyword representations for interpretable product question answering. In *Proceedings of the 25th ACM SIGKDD International Conference on Knowledge Discovery Data Mining*, KDD '19, page 1389–1398, New York, NY, USA. Association for Computing Machinery.

Improving Intent Classification in an E-commerce Voice Assistant by Using Inter-Utterance Context

Arpit Sharma
@WalmartLabs, Sunnyvale, USA
`arpit.sharma@walmartlabs.com`

Abstract

In this work, we improve the intent classification in an English based e-commerce voice assistant by using inter-utterance context. For increased user adaptation and hence being more profitable, an e-commerce voice assistant is desired to understand the context of a conversation and not have the users repeat it in every utterance. For example, let a user's first utterance be *'find apples'*. Then, the user may say *'i want organic only'* to *filter* out the results generated by an assistant with respect to the first query. So, it is important for the assistant to take into account the context from the user's first utterance to understand her intention in the second one. In this paper, we present our approach for contextual intent classification in Walmart's e-commerce voice assistant. It uses the intent of the previous user utterance to predict the intent of her current utterance. With the help of experiments performed on real user queries we show that our approach improves the intent classification in the assistant.

1 Introduction

Recently, there has been a notable advancement in the field of voice assistants[1]. Consequently, voice assistants are being deployed heavily in lucrative domains such as e-commerce (Mari et al., 2020), customer service (Cui et al., 2017) and healthcare (Mavropoulos et al., 2019). There are various e-commerce based voice assistants available in the market, including Amazon's Alexa voice shopping (Maarek, 2018) and Walmart's on Google assistant/Siri[2]. Their goal is to free us from the tedious task of buying stuff by visiting stores and websites. A major challenge in the fulfilment of this goal is their capability to precisely understand an utterance in a dialog without providing much context

in the utterance. For example, an assistant must precisely understand that when a user says *'five'* after a query to *add bananas* to her cart then she intents to *add* five bananas to her cart. Whereas if a user says *'five'* as her first utterance to the shopping assistant then her intention is *unknown* (i.e., it does not represent any e-commerce action at the start of a conversation). Handling such scenarios require the Natural Language Understanding (NLU) component in the assistants to utilize the context while predicting the intent associated with an utterance. The current intent prediction systems (Chen et al., 2019; Goo et al., 2018; Liu and Lane, 2016) do not focus on such contextual dependence. In this work we integrate inter-utterance contextual features in the NLU component of the shopping assistant of Walmart company to improve its intent classification.

There are four main aspects of a voice assistant, namely, Speech-to-Text, NLU, Dialog Management (DM) and Text-to-Speech. The NLU component (such as the one in Liu and Lane (2016)) identifies intent(s) and entities in a user utterance. The dialog manager uses the output of the NLU component to prepare a suitable response for the user. The NLU systems in the currently available voice enabled shopping assistants[3] do not focus on inter-utterance context and hence the onus of context disambiguation lies upon the dialog manager. Although it is possible to capture a small number of such cases in the dialog manager, it becomes difficult for it to scale for large number of contextually dependent utterances. For example, let us consider the user utterance *'five'* after the utterance to add something to her cart. Then a dialog manager can predict its intent by using the rule: *if previous_intent = add_to_cart and the query is an integer then intent = add_to_cart else intent = un-*

---

[1] https://bit.ly/2Xr71xv
[2] https://bit.ly/33TmwkN, https://bit.ly/2JqH9eO
[3] https://bit.ly/2ZAa5KA

Proceedings of the 3rd Workshop on e-Commerce and NLP (ECNLP 3), pages 40–45
Online, July 10, 2020. ©2020 Association for Computational Linguistics

known. But such a general rule can not be created for many other queries such as *'organic please'* (previous intent = *add_to_cart*, intent = *filter*) and *'stop please'* (previous intent = *add_to_cart*, intent = *stop*).

In this paper, we present our work to improve the intent classification in the shopping assistant of Walmart company by using inter-utterance context. Our work also reduces the contextual disambiguation burden from the dialog manager. Here, we implement our approach using two neural network based architectures. With the help of experiments we also compare the two implementations.

2   Related Work

Various intent classification works (Chen et al., 2019; Goo et al., 2018; Liu and Lane, 2016) have been proposed in the recent years. Most of them mainly focus on the current utterance only and try to predict its intent based on the information present in it. We take it one step further and use the context from the immediately previous utterance.

A work which focuses on the contextual information while predicting the intents is mentioned in Naik et al. (2018). It uses visual information as context. Although it is useful in an assistant which comes with a screen, it is not applicable for a voice only assistant.

Another work (Mensio et al., 2018) uses an entire conversation (intents of all the utterances and all the replies from the assistant) as context. Although it makes sense to use the entire conversation as context in a general purpose chat-bot, we believe that in the e-commerce domain a conversation between an assistant and a user is fragmented into smaller goals such as *'finding an item in the inventory'* and *'adding an item in cart'*. Each such goal should be defined by a small number of utterances only. This is because the objective of the voice assistant is to simplify the shopping experience for the user instead of engaging her in a long conversation for a simpler task. So, in our work we use the intent of the previous utterance only as the context for the intent prediction of the current utterance.

3   Data Generation & Our Approach

In this section we provide the data generation details and a detailed overview of our context aware intent classification implementations.

3.1   Contextual Data Generation

In this work our main goal is to improve the intent classification for e-commerce related utterances. We achieve this goal by using inter-utterance context. There are various data sets (ATIS (Hemphill et al., 1990), SNIPS (Coucke et al., 2018)) for intent classification. None of them contain contextual data instances. Furthermore, they do not focus on e-commerce related data. So, as part of this work we generated a context aware data set for e-commerce specific queries. We used a template based approach to generate the data. It was inspired by our previous work as mentioned in Sharma et al. (2018). Following are the two main steps in the data generation phase.

- **Step 1:** A set of 1735 templates (corresponding to 32 intents) are curated over a period of time by product managers and data scientists. An example of a template is "`i wanted [brand]`" where `[brand]` is a placeholder for a product's brand (such as *Shamrock Farms*). The templates are used to generate template and intent combinations. Each such combination contains a previous intent, a template and the template's correct intent. For example, following are two of the combinations generated with respect to the above mentioned template, 1)

  1. previous intent = `search`, template = `i wanted [brand]`, intent = `filter`,
  2. previous intent = `START`, template = `i wanted [brand]`, intent = `unknown`.

- **Step 2:** In this step the placeholders in the template and intent combinations are replaced with their possible values from predefined sets to generate the data points. Multiple data points are generated from each template combination by using the placeholders' values (10 distinct values for each placeholder in each template). The possible values of the placeholders are extracted from the products' catalog of Walmart company.

3.1.1   Fixing Unbalanced Data

The data generated by using the above steps was found to be unbalanced in the following two ways.

1. We found that the generated data contained more instances corresponding to some intents than

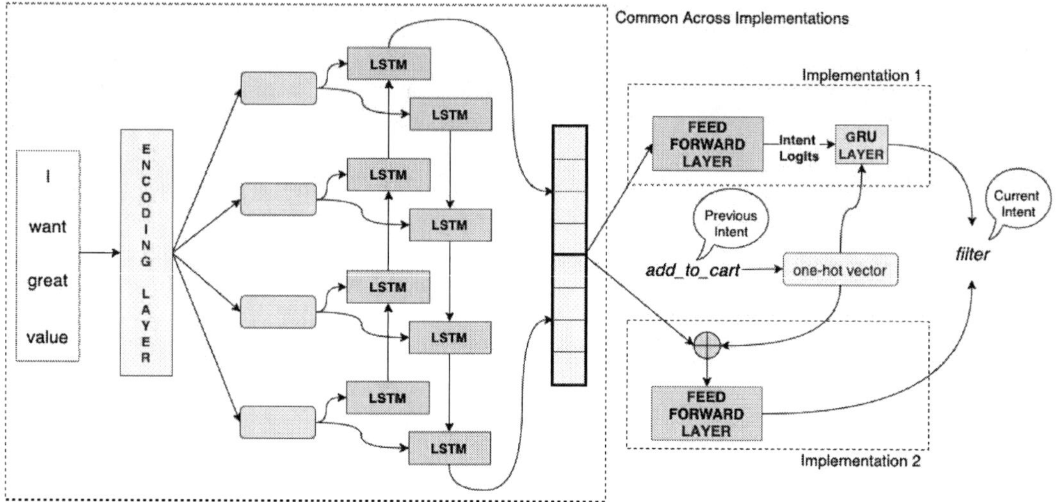

Figure 1: Deep Learning Architectures of the Implementations.
Implementation 1 is Bi-LSTM+FeedForward+GRU and Implementation 2 is Bi-LSTM+FeedForward

others. This is because the templates corresponding to some intents (such as *add to cart*) contained placeholders which were replaced by many possible values whereas the templates corresponding to other intents (such as *stopping a conversation*) did not contain any placeholders. To resolve this kind of skewness we performed Random Oversampling (ROS) (Rathpisey and Adji, 2019) with respect to the intents with minimal data.

2. The contextual instances in the generated data were overwhelmed by their non-contextual parts. Let T be a contextual template such that its intent is I iff the previous intent is P otherwise its intent is unknown. Since there are a total of 32 intents, T corresponds to 32 contextual template combinations of previous intent and current intent. In 31 among those, the current intent of T is unknown whereas only one corresponds to I. To resolve this kind of imbalance we performed Random Oversampling (ROS) (Rathpisey and Adji, 2019) with respect to the one combination mentioned above.

3.2   Our Approach

We used two different neural network architectures for two separate implementations of our approach. The two architectures are as shown in the Figure 1. Following are the details of the architectures.

1. **Bi-LSTM+FeedForward+GRU**: The first architecture is inspired by the work in Mensio et al. (2018). It has two main components. First, a bi-LSTM (Huang et al., 2015; Plank et al., 2016) en-

coder which generates a vector encoding of an input utterance. The vector represents a summarized version of the utterance. It is generated from the embeddings of the words in the query. We experimented with different pre-trained language models (BERT (Devlin et al., 2018) and Glove (Pennington et al., 2014)) to retrieve the initial word embedding. Second component is a GRU (Chung et al., 2014) layer whose inputs consist of the output of a feed forward layer with respect to the embedding generated by the bi-LSTM encoder, along with the one-hot encoding of the previous utterance's intent. The output of this layer is the intent of the input utterance (See Figure 1).

2. **Bi-LSTM+FeedForward**: Similar to the first architecture, the second one also has two components, a bi-LSTM layer followed by a feed forward layer. As in the first architecture, the bi-LSTM layer generates a vector which represents a user utterance. The output of the bi-LSTM layer is then concatenated with the one-hot encoding of the previous intent and entered as an input to a feed forward layer (See Figure 1).

4   Evaluation & Results

The main goal of this work is to improve the intent classification in the NLU component of Walmart's shopping assistant by using inter-utterance context. In this section we present the quantitative details of the data, the experiments and the analysis of the results.

Implementation	Oversampling	Intent Accuracy on User Logs (% correct)		
		Glove 6B	Glove 840B	BERT
Bi-LSTM+FeedForward+GRU	✔	83.05	80.51	**87.68**
	✘	79.12	73.64	72.98
Bi-LSTM+FeedForward	✔	86.5	86.67	86.34
	✘	82.58	83.39	70.57

Table 1: Evaluation results for Contextual Intent Classification on 2550 Real User Queries

4.1 Dataset Details

We followed the data generation steps mentioned in the Section 3.1 with and without oversampling to generate a set of 730K and 570K instances respectively. Each set is split into training (85%) and validation (15%). For testing the trained models we used the real user queries which were taken from the live logs of Walmart's shopping assistant. We selected all the queries from two weeks of live logs. Then we filtered the retrieved queries by keeping only the unique ones. By following the above steps, we got 2550 unique user queries in our test set.

4.2 Experiment 1

The hypothesis that led to this work states that contextual evidence is needed to find the correct intent of a user utterance in an e-commerce voice assistant. To test the hypothesis, in this experiment we analyzed the set of 2550 unique user utterances from user logs. 40.11% of those (i.e., 1023) were found to be contextual. For example *'give me a smaller size'* is one such contextual query which when appears after an *add to cart* utterance, implies *filtering* the results of the previous utterance whereas when appeared first in a conversation between a user and a voice assistant, does not make sense (or *unknown* intent). The *add to cart* and *search* intents are most popular among the logs. We found that 1005 out of 1023 contextual queries were related to those intents. This emphasizes the importance of contextual disambiguation even further. 917 (approx. 90%) among 1023 were correctly classified by the best performing version (BERT based) of our implementations (see Table 1). The current, non-contextual intent classifier of the Walmart's shopping assistant classifies all the contextual queries as one intent (say *abc*). The contextual disambiguation burden lies on the dialog manager by using rules (as mentioned in the Section 1). Presently, a total of 12 rules exist to handle contextual templates corresponding to one intent (out of 32) only. We also found that out of 1023

contextual queries, about 88% are classified by the non-contextual intent classifier as *abc*.

4.3 Experiment 2

In this experiment, we tested our implementations with respect to different input word embedding and data (with oversampling and without oversampling). We used BERT's huggingface[4] pretrained embedding (length=768), and Glove[5] 6 billion and 840 billion pre-trained embedding (length=300). The evaluation results are as shown in the Table 1. Each model was trained for 10 epochs. The BERT embedding of a word was calculated by taking an average of the last 4 layers in the 12-layer BERT pre-trained model[5].

4.4 Results Analysis

The results of experiment 1 show the usefulness of contextual intent classification.

The results of experiment 2 show that the Bi-LSTM and GRU based implementation performs best with an overall accuracy of 87.68% on all the live user logs and approximately 90% on the contextual logs.

Inference speed plays an important role in production deployment of models. Although the performance of BERT based Bi-LSTM+FeedForward+GRU is better than the Glove (840B) based Bi-LSTM+FeedForward, the latency of first (450 milliseconds, averaged over 2550 queries on CPU) one is considerably more than the second (5 milliseconds on CPU). See Table 2 for inference speeds of the different models.

We observed that many (about 50%) errors in both the implementations were caused by the inability of the training data to represent real user data. A way to address such errors is by using real user queries also to train the models. It requires manual effort to label user logs. We are currently in the process of such an effort through crowd workers.

---

[4]https://github.com/huggingface/transformers
[5]https://nlp.stanford.edu/projects/glove/

Implementation	Word Embedding	Inference Speed (CPU)
Bi-LSTM+FeedForward+GRU	Glove 6B	≈ 5 ms
Bi-LSTM+FeedForward+GRU	Glove 840B	≈ 5 ms
Bi-LSTM+FeedForward+GRU	BERT	≈ 450 ms
Bi-LSTM+FeedForward	Glove 6B	≈ 5 ms
Bi-LSTM+FeedForward	Glove 840B	≈ 5 ms
Bi-LSTM+FeedForward	BERT	≈ 450 ms

Table 2: Inference Speed of Different Models (Averaged Over 2550 Real User Queries)

We believe that using a combination of templates based and real user data will improve the accuracy of the implementations even further.

5 Conclusion & Future Work

In this paper, we presented our work of improving intent classification in Walmart's shopping assistant. We used previous utterance's intent as context to identify current utterance's intent. The contextual update in the NLU layer (intent classification) also takes the burden of intent based contextual disambiguation away from a dialog manager. As hypothesized, the experimental results show that our approach improves the intent classification by handling contextual queries. We presented two implementations of our approach and compared them with respect to live user logs.

Though, in this work our main focus was on the contextual disambiguation of intents, the entities are also contextually dependent. For example *'five'* uttered after *'add bananas'* may refer to the quantity *five* whereas if uttered after *'pick a delivery time'* may refer to the time of day *five (am/pm)*. In future we would like to use contextual features to disambiguate between entities and improve the entity tagging as well.

Acknowledgments

I would like to acknowledge the support of my colleagues in the Emerging Technologies team at WalmartLabs, Sunnyvale, CA office. They provided their valuable feedback which helped in maturing this submission to a publishable states.

References

Qian Chen, Zhu Zhuo, and Wen Wang. 2019. Bert for joint intent classification and slot filling. *arXiv preprint arXiv:1902.10909*.

Junyoung Chung, Caglar Gulcehre, KyungHyun Cho, and Yoshua Bengio. 2014. Empirical evaluation of gated recurrent neural networks on sequence modeling. *arXiv preprint arXiv:1412.3555*.

Alice Coucke, Alaa Saade, Adrien Ball, Théodore Bluche, Alexandre Caulier, David Leroy, Clément Doumouro, Thibault Gisselbrecht, Francesco Caltagirone, Thibaut Lavril, et al. 2018. Snips voice platform: an embedded spoken language understanding system for private-by-design voice interfaces. *arXiv preprint arXiv:1805.10190*.

Lei Cui, Shaohan Huang, Furu Wei, Chuanqi Tan, Chaoqun Duan, and Ming Zhou. 2017. Superagent: A customer service chatbot for e-commerce websites. In *Proceedings of ACL 2017, System Demonstrations*, pages 97–102.

Jacob Devlin, Ming-Wei Chang, Kenton Lee, and Kristina Toutanova. 2018. Bert: Pre-training of deep bidirectional transformers for language understanding. *arXiv preprint arXiv:1810.04805*.

Chih-Wen Goo, Guang Gao, Yun-Kai Hsu, Chih-Li Huo, Tsung-Chieh Chen, Keng-Wei Hsu, and Yun-Nung Chen. 2018. Slot-gated modeling for joint slot filling and intent prediction. In *Proceedings of the 2018 Conference of the North American Chapter of the Association for Computational Linguistics: Human Language Technologies, Volume 2 (Short Papers)*, pages 753–757.

Charles T Hemphill, John J Godfrey, and George R Doddington. 1990. The atis spoken language systems pilot corpus. In *Speech and Natural Language: Proceedings of a Workshop Held at Hidden Valley, Pennsylvania, June 24-27, 1990*.

Zhiheng Huang, Wei Xu, and Kai Yu. 2015. Bidirectional lstm-crf models for sequence tagging. *arXiv preprint arXiv:1508.01991*.

Bing Liu and Ian Lane. 2016. Attention-based recurrent neural network models for joint intent detection and slot filling. *arXiv preprint arXiv:1609.01454*.

Yoelle Maarek. 2018. Alexa and her shopping journey. In *Proceedings of the 27th ACM International Conference on Information and Knowledge Management*, pages 1–1.

Alex Mari, Andreina Mandelli, and René Algesheimer. 2020. The evolution of marketing in the context of voice commerce: A managerial perspective. In *Proceeding of the 22nd International Conference on Human-Computer Interaction.*

Thanassis Mavropoulos, Georgios Meditskos, Spyridon Symeonidis, Eleni Kamateri, Maria Rousi, Dimitris Tzimikas, Lefteris Papageorgiou, Christos Eleftheriadis, George Adamopoulos, Stefanos Vrochidis, et al. 2019. A context-aware conversational agent in the rehabilitation domain. *Future Internet*, 11(11):231.

Martino Mensio, Giuseppe Rizzo, and Maurizio Morisio. 2018. Multi-turn qa: A rnn contextual approach to intent classification for goal-oriented systems. In *Companion Proceedings of the The Web Conference 2018*, pages 1075–1080.

Vishal Ishwar Naik, Angeliki Metallinou, and Rahul Goel. 2018. Context aware conversational understanding for intelligent agents with a screen. In *Thirty-Second AAAI Conference on Artificial Intelligence.*

Jeffrey Pennington, Richard Socher, and Christopher D Manning. 2014. Glove: Global vectors for word representation. In *Proceedings of the 2014 conference on empirical methods in natural language processing (EMNLP)*, pages 1532–1543.

Barbara Plank, Anders Søgaard, and Yoav Goldberg. 2016. Multilingual part-of-speech tagging with bidirectional long short-term memory models and auxiliary loss. *arXiv preprint arXiv:1604.05529.*

Heng Rathpisey and Teguh Bharata Adji. 2019. Handling imbalance issue in hate speech classification using sampling-based methods. In *2019 5th International Conference on Science in Information Technology (ICSITech)*, pages 193–198. IEEE.

Arpit Sharma, Vivek Kaul, and Shankara B Subramanya. 2018. Semantic representation and parsing for voice ecommerce. In *R2K Workshop: Integrating learning of Representations and models with deductive Reasoning that leverages Knowledge (Co-located with KR 2018).*

Semi-Supervised Iterative Approach for Domain-Specific Complaint Detection in Social Media

Akash Gautam
MIDAS, IIIT-Delhi
akash15011@iiitd.ac.in

Debanjan Mahata
Bloomberg, New York, U.S.A
dmahata@bloomberg.net

Rakesh Gosangi
Bloomberg, New York, U.S.A
rgosangi@bloomberg.net

Rajiv Ratn Shah
MIDAS, IIIT-Delhi
rajivratn@iiitd.ac.in

Abstract

In this paper, we present a semi-supervised bootstrapping approach to detect product or service related complaints in social media. Our approach begins with a small collection of annotated samples which are used to identify a preliminary set of linguistic indicators pertinent to complaints. These indicators are then used to expand the dataset. The expanded dataset is again used to extract more indicators. This process is applied for several iterations until we can no longer find any new indicators. We evaluated this approach on a Twitter corpus specifically to detect complaints about transportation services. We started with an annotated set of 326 samples of transportation complaints, and after four iterations of the approach, we collected 2,840 indicators and over 3,700 tweets. We annotated a random sample of 700 tweets from the final dataset and observed that nearly half the samples were actual transportation complaints. Lastly, we also studied how different features based on semantics, orthographic properties, and sentiment contribute towards the prediction of complaints.

1 Introduction

Social media has lately become one of the primary venues where users express their opinions about various products and services. These opinions are extremely useful in understanding the user's perceptions and sentiment about these services. They are also useful in identifying potential defects (Abrahams et al., 2012) and thus critical to the execution of downstream customer service responses. Therefore, automatic detection of user complaints on social media could prove beneficial to both the clients and the service providers. To build such detection systems, we could employ supervised approaches that would typically require a large corpus of labeled training samples. However,

labeling social media posts that capture complaints about a particular service is challenging because of their low prevalence and also the vast amounts of inevitable noise (Kietzmann et al., 2011; Lee, 2018). Additionally, social media platforms are also likely to be plagued with redundancy, where the posts are rephrased or structurally morphed before being re-posted (Ellison et al., 2011; Harrigan et al., 2012).

Prior work in event detection (Ritter et al., 2012) has demonstrated that simple linguistic indicators (phrases or n-grams) can be useful in the accurate discovery of events in social media. Though user complaints are not the same as events, more of a speech act (Preotiuc-Pietro et al., 2019), we posit that similar indicators can be used in complaint detection. To pursue this hypothesis, we propose a semi-supervised iterative approach to identify social media posts that complain about a specific service.

In our approach, we first begin with a small, manually curated dataset containing samples of social media posts complaining about a service. We then identify linguistic indicators (phrases or n-grams) that serve as strong evidence of this phenomenon. These indicators are then used to extract more posts from the unannotated corpus. This newly obtained data is then used to create a new set of indicators. This process is repeated until it reaches a certain convergence point. Since the set of indicators is growing after each iteration, they are re-evaluated continuously in terms of their relevance. This process is similar to the mutual bootstrapping approach for information extraction proposed in (Riloff et al., 2003).

We employ this approach to the problem of complaint detection for transportation services on Twitter. Transportation and its related logistic services are critical aspects of every economy as they account for nearly 40% of the value of international

Proceedings of the 3rd Workshop on e-Commerce and NLP (ECNLP 3), pages 46–53
Online, July 10, 2020. ©2020 Association for Computational Linguistics

trade (Rodrigue, 2007). As with most businesses (Gallaugher and Ransbotham, 2010; Gottipati et al., 2018), transportation also often relies on social media to ascertain feedback and initiate appropriate responses (Stelzer et al., 2016, 2014). In our experimental work, we started with an annotated set of 326 samples of transportation complaints, and after four iterations of the approach, we collected 2,840 indicators and over 3,700 tweets. We annotated a random sample of 700 tweets from the final dataset and observed that over 47% of the samples were actual transportation complaints. We also characterize the performance of basic classification algorithms on this dataset. In doing so, we also study how different linguistic features contribute to the performance of a supervised model in this domain.

The main contributions of this paper are as follows:

- We propose a semi-supervised iterative approach to collect user complaints about a service from social media platforms.

- We evaluate the proposed approach for the problem of complaint detection for transportation services on Twitter.

- We annotate a random sample of the resulting dataset to establish that nearly half the tweets were actual complaints.

- We release a curated dataset for the task of traffic-related complaint detection in social media[1].

- Lastly, we characterize the performance of basic classification algorithms on the dataset.

2 Related Work

Complaints are often considered dialogue acts used to express a mismatch between the expectation and reality (Olshtain and Weinbach, 1985). The problem of complaint detection is of great interest to the marketing and research teams of various service providers. Previous works on complaint identification have applied text mining with LDA and sentiment analysis on user-generated content (Liu et al., 2017; Duan et al., 2013). Prior works have also focused on leveraging data streamed from social

media platforms for *outage* and complaint detection as they are publicly available (Augustine et al., 2012; Kursar and Gopinath, 2013).

(Yang et al., 2019) inspected customer support dialogue for support. Different complaint expressions have been explored by analyzing variations across cultures (Cohen and Olshtain, 1993), socio-demographic traits (Boxer, 1993) and temporal representations (Raghavan, 2014). However, mentioned works on user-generated content have focused on static data repositories only. These have not been robust to linguistic variations (Shah and Zimmermann, 2017) and morphological changes (Abdul-Mageed and Korayem, 2010). Our pipeline builds on linguistic identifiers to expand on lexical cues in order to identify complaint relevant posts.

Researches have proposed many semi-supervised architectures for identification of events pertaining to societal and civil unrest (Hua et al., 2013), using speech modality (Serizel et al., 2018; Wu et al., 2014; Zhang et al., 2017) and Hidden Markov Models (Zhang, 2005). These have been documented to give better performance as compared against their counterparts (Lee et al., 2017; Zheng et al., 2017) with minimal intervention (Rahimi et al., 2018). For our analysis, the semi-supervised approach has been preferred as opposed to supervised ones because: (a) usage of supervised approach relies on carefully choosing the training set making it cumbersome and less attractive for practical use (Watanabe, 2018) and (b) imbalance between the subjective and objective classes lead to poor performance (Yu et al., 2015).

3 Methods and Data

Our proposed approach begins with a large corpus of transport-related tweets and a small set of annotated complaints. We use this labeled data to create a set of *seed* indicators that drive the rest of our iterative complaint detection process.

3.1 Seed Data

We focused our experimentation over the period of November 2018 to December 2018. Our first step towards creating a corpus of transport-related tweets is to identify linguistic markers related to the transport domain. To this end, we scraped random posts from transport-related web forums[2]. These forums involve users discussing their grievances and raising awareness about a wide

---

array of transportation-related issues. We then processed this data to extract words and phrases (unigrams, bigrams, and trigrams) with high tf-idf scores. We then had human annotators prune them further to remove duplicates and irrelevant items. This resulted in a lexicon of 75 unique phrases. Some examples include *cabs, discount, tickets, underground, luggage, transit, parking, neighborhood, downtown, traffic, Uber.*

We used Twitter's public streaming API to query for tweets that contained any of the 75 phrases over the chosen time range. We then excluded non-English tweets and any tweets with less than two tokens. This resulted in a collection of 19,300 tweets. We will refer to this collection as corpus C. We chose a random sample of 1,500 tweets from this collection for human annotation. We employed two human annotators to identify traffic-related complaints from these 1,500 tweets. Following are some high-level details of the annotation task.

We instructed the annotators to identify any tweets that contain first-hand accounts of a complaint or a grievance related to a public/private mode of transport. Following is a sample tweet from this instruction: *"@[UserHandle] can you please make sure that compartment A-6 is at least clean before public use."* We also instructed them to identify tweets that provide verifiable sources of information (news) about transport-related services. Sample tweet: *"4 hour jam in [place] area due to rain and poor management of traffic police."*. Lastly, we also explicitly asked them to exclude tweets that contain announcements or advertisements about transportation services. Sample tweet: *"Please use [name] cabs, you will get 60% discount on your first 3 rides."*

The two annotators worked independently, and when we finally tallied their responses, we observed that they had an inter-annotator agreement rate of $\kappa = 0.81$ (Cohen kappa). In cases where the annotators disagreed, the labels were resolved through a discussion. After the disagreements were resolved, the final seed dataset had 326 samples of traffic-related complaints. We will refer to this as T_s. Table 1 shows some examples of tweets that were annotated as complaints.

3.2 Iterative Complaint Detection

Our proposed iterative approach is summarized in Algorithm 1. First, we use the seed data T_s to build a set of linguistic indicators I for complaints.

We then use these indicators to get potential new complaints T_l from the corpus C. We merge T_s and T_l to build our new dataset. We then use this new dataset to extract a new set of indicators I_l. The indicators are combined with the original indicators I to extract the next version of T_l. This process is repeated until we can no longer find any new indicators.

Algorithm 1: Iterative Complaint Detection

Given: Corpus: C, Seed data: T_s
Get indicators I from T_s
$T = T_s$
Complaint Detection loop
Step 1: Select set T_l from C using I
Step 2: $T = T \cup T_l$
Step 3: Get indicators I_l from T
Step 4: $I = I \cup I_l$
Step 4: $C = C - T_l$

3.2.1 Extracting linguistic indicators

As shown in Algorithm 1, extracting linguistic indicators (n-grams) is one of the most important steps in the process. These indicators are critical to identifying tweets that are most likely domain-specific complaints. We employ two different approaches for extracting these indicators. For seed data, T_s, which is annotated, we just select n-grams with the highest tf-idf scores. In our experimental work, T_s had 326 annotated tweets. We identified 50 n-grams with the highest tf-idf scores to initialize I. Some examples include: ***problem, station, services, toll-fee, reply, fault, provide information, driver, district, passenger***. In subsequent iterations, when we are handling unannotated samples, we use a more advanced **domain relevance** criterion for extracting the indicators.

When extracting indicators from T_l, which is not annotated, it is possible that there could be frequently occurring phrases that are not necessarily indicative of complaints. These phrases could lead to a concept drift in subsequent iterations. To avoid these digressions, we use a measure of **domain relevance** when selecting indicators. This is defined as the ratio of the frequency of an n-gram in T_l to that of in T_r. T_r is a collection of randomly chosen tweets that do not intersect with C. In our experimental work, we defined T_r as a random sample of 5,000 tweets from a different time range than that of C. We also wanted to quantitatively en-

Samples of transport-related complaints.
1. *No metro fares will be reduced, but proper fare structure needs to be introduced .... right?.*
2. *It takes [name] govt. longer to refund charges, but it took them a few mins to remove that bus stop. You can't erase the problem[name].*
3. *I tried to lodge a complaint on [url] but see the results. Sir if 8 A.C's are not working in this coach , why have you attached that coach.*
4. *[name] Is that for when people can't travel due to your staff having to strike to keep everyone safe? Or perhaps short formed trains that you cant get on.*

Table 1: Sample tweets annotated as transport-related complaints.

sure that the lexicon in T_r is different from that of C. Namely, we calculated the cosine similarity between the two datasets in the tf-idf space. The cosine similarity at a value of 0.028 was statistically significant with a Pearson correlation coefficient value 0.012 (*p-value 0.0034*) (Schober et al., 2018).

3.2.2   Selection of tweets

Given a set of indicators I, the process of selecting tweets from corpus C is fairly straightforward. It only requires to identify all the tweet that contains any of the indicators. The only caveat here is to reduce the redundancy in the dataset. For this, we just filtered out tweets that have a cosine similarity of more than 0.85 with any other tweet in the tf-idf space (Albakour et al., 2013). This process also helped remove tweets, which are exact matches, sub-strings, or differing by some punctuation. Removal of these redundant tweets also helps in diversifying the lexicon for subsequent iterations.

3.2.3   Complaints dataset

Our iterative approach converged in four rounds, after which it did not extract any new indicators. Figure 1 shows the counts of indicators and the number of tweets after each iteration. After four iterations, this approach chose 3,732 tweets and generated 2,840 unique indicators. We also manually inspected the indicators chosen during the process. We observed that only indicators with a domain relevance score of ≥ 2.5 were chosen for subsequent iterations. Table 2 provides a few examples of strong and weak indicators acquired after the first iteration. In this figure, strong indicators are those with a domain relevance score ≥ 2.5.

We chose a random set of 700 tweets from the final complaints dataset T and annotated them manually to help understand the quality. We used the same guidelines as discussed in section 3.1 and also employed the same annotators as before. The anno-

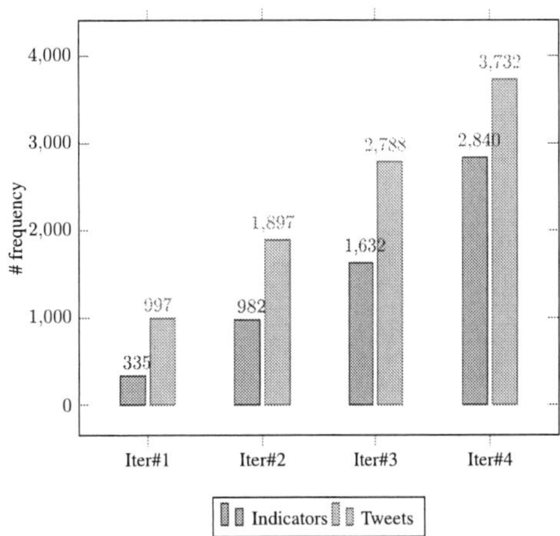

Figure 1: Number of indicators and tweets collected after each iteration.

tators once again obtained a high agreement score of $\kappa = 0.83$. After resolving the disagreements, we observed that 332 tweets were labeled as complaints. This accounts for 47.4% of the sampled 700 tweets. This demonstrates that nearly half the tweets selected by our semi-supervised approach were traffic-related complaints. This is a significantly higher proportion in the original seed data T_s, where only 21.7% were actual complaints.

4   Modeling

We conducted a series of experiments to understand if we can automatically build simple machine learning models to detect complaints. These experiments also helped us evaluate the quality of the final dataset. Additionally, this experimental work also studies how different types of linguistic features contribute to the detection of social media complaints. For these experiments, we used the annotated sample of 700 posts as a test dataset. We built our training dataset by selecting another 2,000 posts from the original corpus C, and anno-

Strength	Indicator
Strong	car travel (*5.80*), your complaint (*3.62*), technical problem (*3.59*), report officer (*3.44*), traffic control (*3.33*), make apologies(*3.29*)
Weak	you go (*0.55*), sure (*0.51*), please (*0.49*), take this (*0.44*), with you (*0.42*), therefore (*0.39*), make him (*0.36*)

Table 2: Examples of some strong and weak indicators. The numbers in brackets denote the respective domain relevance score.

Feature	Accuracy(%)	F1-score
Semantic Features		
Unigrams	**75.3**	**0.70**
POS Tags	70.1	0.66
Word2Vec cluster	72.1	0.67
Pronoun Types	69.6	0.65
Sentiment Features		
MPQA	68.2	0.61
NRC	67.9	0.59
VADER	68.0	0.62
Stanford Sentiment	68.7	0.63
Orthographic Features		
Textual Meta-data	69.3	0.62
Intensifiers	72.5	0.67
Request Features		
Request Model	70.1	0.66
Politeness Markers	70.4	0.63

Table 3: Predictive accuracy and F1-score associated with different types of features.

tated them once again per guidelines discussed in section 3.1. In this sample, we observed that the annotators had similar agreements scores of $\kappa = 0.79$, and there were 702 instances of complaints.

4.1 Features

We also wanted to understand the predictive power of different types of linguistic features towards the detection of complaints. These features can be broadly broken down into four groups. (i) The first group of features are based on simple semantic properties such as *n-grams*, *word embeddings*, and *part of speech tags*. (ii) The second group of features are based on *pre-trained sentiment models* or *lexicons*. (iii) The third group of features use *orthographic information* such as *hashtags*, *user mentions*, and *intensifiers*. (iv) The last group of features again use *pre-trained models* or *lexicons* associated with *request*, which is a closely related speech act (Švárová, 2008).

4.1.1 Semantic features

We experimented with four different semantic features:

Unigrams: Each tweet (Wallach, 2006) is represented as sparse vector of tf-idf values correspond-

ing to the constituent tokens.

Word2Vec Clusters: We follow the same approach as in (Preoţiuc-Pietro et al., 2015), where words are clustered using pair-wise similarities in Word2Vec space (Mikolov et al., 2013). Each tweet is then represented as a distribution over these clusters; the values are proportional to the number of tokens belonging to a cluster. These clusters have previously been demonstrated to have great interpretability (Preoţiuc-Pietro et al., 2015, 2017; Zou et al., 2016).

POS Tags: We used the Stanford POS Tagger (Manning et al., 2014) to represent tweets as a dense frequency vector over five main POS tags: *nouns, adjectives, adverbs, verbs, pronouns*.

Pronoun Types: Pronouns are often used in complaints and suggestions to reveal personal involvement or to add intensity to an opinion (Claridge, 2007; Meinl, 2013). We identify various pronoun types (*first person, second person, third person, demonstrative, indefinite*) using dictionaries and use their counts as features.

4.1.2 Sentiment features

We expect sentiment to contribute strongly towards the prediction of complaints. We experiment with two *pre-trained models*: Stanford Sentiment (Socher et al., 2013) and VADER (Hutto and Gilbert, 2014). Namely, we use the scores predicted by these models as representations of tweets. Likewise, we also experiment with two sentiment lexicons: MPQA (Wilson et al., 2005), NRC (Mohammad et al., 2013) for assigning sentiment scores to tweets.

4.1.3 Orthographic features

Our first set of orthographic feature uses counts of URLs, hashtags, user mentions, and special symbols used in the post. The second set of orthographic features try to identify potential intensifiers such as capitalization and repeated use of exclamation or question marks. These types of intensifiers are often used to express anger or strong opinions

(Meinl, 2013).

4.1.4 Request features

A request is a speech act very closely related to complaints. Often, the main motivation behind a complaint on a social media platform is to get a correction or reparation from the service providers (Blum-Kulka and Olshtain, 1984). We use the model presented in (Danescu-Niculescu-Mizil et al., 2013) to detect if a given tweet is a *request*. Requests might also often include polite phrases in expectation of better service. They are coded using various dictionaries e.g, downgraders (*little*), down-toners (*just*), hedges (*somewhat*). Apology markers have the same effect as politeness markers, they may include greetings at the start (*Good Morning*), direct start (*e.g so*), subjunctive phrases (*could you*) (Švárová, 2008). We utilize pre-defined dictionaries to determine the presence of politeness identifiers along with the politeness score of the tweet based on the model in (Danescu-Niculescu-Mizil et al., 2013).

4.2 Results

We trained a logistic regression model for complaint detection using each one of the features described in section 4.1. Table 3 summarizes the results in terms of accuracy and macro averaged F1-score. The best performing model is based on unigrams, with an accuracy of 75.3%. There is not a significant difference in the performance of different sentiment models. It is also interesting to observe that simple features like the counts of different pronoun types and counts of intensifiers have strong predictive ability. Overall, we observe that most of the features studied here have some ability to predict complaints.

5 Conclusion and Future Work

In this paper, we presented a semi-supervised iterative approach for the detection of complaints in social media platforms. The process begins with a small sample of annotated examples, and then iteratively builds more linguistic identifiers to expand the dataset. We evaluated this approach on the domain of transportation on Twitter, starting with a sample of 326 annotated tweets. After four iterations, we were able to construct a corpus with over 3,700 tweets. Annotation of random samples established that nearly half the tweets were actual complaints. We evaluated the predictive power based on semantic, orthographic, and sentiment features. We observed that complaint is a complex speech act, which is related to many other linguistic properties.

Automatic detection of complaints is not only useful to service providers as feedback; it could also prove helpful in improving service providers' operations and in downstream applications such as developing chat-bots. Additionally, it could also be of interest to linguists in understanding how humans express grievances and criticism.

This proposed methodology could be applied to many other products or services to detect complaints. This would only additionally require some lexicons and a small annotated dataset. We also expect it would be fairly straightforward to adapt this technique to many other types of speech acts. Further investigation is necessary to understand how this method compares against supervised or completely unsupervised techniques.

References

Muhammad Abdul-Mageed and Mohammed Korayem. 2010. Automatic identification of subjectivity in morphologically rich languages: the case of arabic. *Computational approaches to subjectivity and sentiment analysis*, 2:2–6.

Alan S Abrahams, Jian Jiao, G Alan Wang, and Weiguo Fan. 2012. Vehicle defect discovery from social media. *Decision Support Systems*, 54(1):87–97.

M Albakour, Craig Macdonald, Iadh Ounis, et al. 2013. On sparsity and drift for effective real-time filtering in microblogs. In *Proceedings of the 22nd ACM international conference on Information & Knowledge Management*, pages 419–428. ACM.

Eriq Augustine, Cailin Cushing, Alex Dekhtyar, Kevin McEntee, Kimberly Paterson, and Matt Tognetti. 2012. Outage detection via real-time social stream analysis: leveraging the power of online complaints. In *Proceedings of the 21st International Conference on World Wide Web*, pages 13–22.

Shoshana Blum-Kulka and Elite Olshtain. 1984. Requests and apologies: A cross-cultural study of speech act realization patterns (ccsarp). *Applied linguistics*, 5(3):196–213.

Diana Boxer. 1993. Social distance and speech behavior: The case of indirect complaints. *Journal of pragmatics*, 19(2):103–125.

Claudia Claridge. 2007. The superlative in spoken english. In *Corpus Linguistics 25 Years on*, pages 121–148. Brill Rodopi.

Andrew D Cohen and Elite Olshtain. 1993. The production of speech acts by efl learners. *Tesol Quarterly*, 27(1):33–56.

Cristian Danescu-Niculescu-Mizil, Robert West, Dan Jurafsky, Jure Leskovec, and Christopher Potts. 2013. No country for old members: User lifecycle and linguistic change in online communities. In *Proceedings of the 22nd international conference on World Wide Web*, pages 307–318. ACM.

Wenjing Duan, Qing Cao, Yang Yu, and Stuart Levy. 2013. Mining online user-generated content: using sentiment analysis technique to study hotel service quality. In *2013 46th Hawaii International Conference on System Sciences*, pages 3119–3128. IEEE.

Nicole B Ellison, Jessica Vitak, Charles Steinfield, Rebecca Gray, and Cliff Lampe. 2011. Negotiating privacy concerns and social capital needs in a social media environment. In *Privacy online*, pages 19–32. Springer.

John Gallaugher and Sam Ransbotham. 2010. Social media and customer dialog management at starbucks. *MIS Quarterly Executive*, 9(4).

Swapna Gottipati, Venky Shankararaman, and Jeff Rongsheng Lin. 2018. Text analytics approach to extract course improvement suggestions from students' feedback. *Research and Practice in Technology Enhanced Learning*, 13(1):6.

Nicholas Harrigan, Palakorn Achananuparp, and Ee-Peng Lim. 2012. Influentials, novelty, and social contagion: The viral power of average friends, close communities, and old news. *Social Networks*, 34(4):470–480.

Ting Hua, Feng Chen, Liang Zhao, Chang-Tien Lu, and Naren Ramakrishnan. 2013. Sted: semi-supervised targeted-interest event detectionin in twitter. In *Proceedings of the 19th ACM SIGKDD international conference on Knowledge discovery and data mining*, pages 1466–1469.

Clayton J Hutto and Eric Gilbert. 2014. Vader: A parsimonious rule-based model for sentiment analysis of social media text. In *Eighth international AAAI conference on weblogs and social media*.

Jan H Kietzmann, Kristopher Hermkens, Ian P McCarthy, and Bruno S Silvestre. 2011. Social media? get serious! understanding the functional building blocks of social media. *Business horizons*, 54(3):241–251.

Brian Kursar and Jayadev Gopinath. 2013. Validating customer complaints based on social media postings. US Patent App. 13/646,548.

In Lee. 2018. Social media analytics for enterprises: Typology, methods, and processes. *Business Horizons*, 61(2):199–210.

Kathy Lee, Ashequl Qadir, Sadid A Hasan, Vivek Datla, Aaditya Prakash, Joey Liu, and Oladimeji Farri. 2017. Adverse drug event detection in tweets with semi-supervised convolutional neural networks. In *Proceedings of the 26th International Conference on World Wide Web*, pages 705–714.

Xia Liu, Alvin C Burns, and Yingjian Hou. 2017. An investigation of brand-related user-generated content on twitter. *Journal of Advertising*, 46(2):236–247.

Christopher Manning, Mihai Surdeanu, John Bauer, Jenny Finkel, Steven Bethard, and David McClosky. 2014. The stanford corenlp natural language processing toolkit. In *Proceedings of 52nd annual meeting of the association for computational linguistics: system demonstrations*, pages 55–60.

Marja E Meinl. 2013. *Electronic complaints: an empirical study on British English and German complaints on eBay*, volume 18. Frank & Timme GmbH.

Tomas Mikolov, Kai Chen, Greg Corrado, and Jeffrey Dean. 2013. Efficient estimation of word representations in vector space. *arXiv preprint arXiv:1301.3781*.

Saif M Mohammad, Svetlana Kiritchenko, and Xiaodan Zhu. 2013. Nrc-canada: Building the state-of-the-art in sentiment analysis of tweets. *arXiv preprint arXiv:1308.6242*.

Elite Olshtain and Liora Weinbach. 1985. *Complaints-A study of speech act behavior among native and nonnative speakers of Hebrew*. Tel Aviv University.

Daniel Preotiuc-Pietro, Mihaela Gaman, and Nikolaos Aletras. 2019. Automatically identifying complaints in social media. *arXiv preprint arXiv:1906.03890*.

Daniel Preoţiuc-Pietro, Vasileios Lampos, and Nikolaos Aletras. 2015. An analysis of the user occupational class through twitter content. In *Proceedings of the 53rd Annual Meeting of the Association for Computational Linguistics and the 7th International Joint Conference on Natural Language Processing (Volume 1: Long Papers)*, volume 1, pages 1754–1764.

Daniel Preoţiuc-Pietro, Ye Liu, Daniel Hopkins, and Lyle Ungar. 2017. Beyond binary labels: political ideology prediction of twitter users. In *Proceedings of the 55th Annual Meeting of the Association for Computational Linguistics (Volume 1: Long Papers)*, pages 729–740.

Preethi Raghavan. 2014. *Medical event timeline generation from clinical narratives*. Ph.D. thesis, The Ohio State University.

Afshin Rahimi, Trevor Cohn, and Timothy Baldwin. 2018. Semi-supervised user geolocation via graph convolutional networks. *arXiv preprint arXiv:1804.08049*.

Ellen Riloff, Janyce Wiebe, and Theresa Wilson. 2003. Learning subjective nouns using extraction pattern bootstrapping. In *Proceedings of the Seventh Conference on Natural Language Learning at HLT-NAACL 2003*, pages 25–32.

Alan Ritter, Oren Etzioni, Sam Clark, et al. 2012. Open domain event extraction from twitter. In *Proceedings of the 18th ACM SIGKDD international conference on Knowledge discovery and data mining*, pages 1104–1112. ACM.

Jean-Paul Rodrigue. 2007. Transportation and globalization. *Encyclopedia of.*

Patrick Schober, Christa Boer, and Lothar A Schwarte. 2018. Correlation coefficients: appropriate use and interpretation. *Anesthesia & Analgesia*, 126(5):1763–1768.

Romain Serizel, Nicolas Turpault, Hamid Eghbal-Zadeh, and Ankit Parag Shah. 2018. Large-scale weakly labeled semi-supervised sound event detection in domestic environments. *arXiv preprint arXiv:1807.10501.*

Rajiv Shah and Roger Zimmermann. 2017. *Multimodal analysis of user-generated multimedia content.* Springer.

Richard Socher, Alex Perelygin, Jean Wu, Jason Chuang, Christopher D Manning, Andrew Ng, and Christopher Potts. 2013. Recursive deep models for semantic compositionality over a sentiment treebank. In *Proceedings of the 2013 conference on empirical methods in natural language processing*, pages 1631–1642.

Anselmo Stelzer, Frank Englert, Stephan Hörold, and Cindy Mayas. 2014. Using customer feedback in public transportation systems. In *2014 International Conference on Advanced Logistics and Transport (ICALT)*, pages 29–34. IEEE.

Anselmo Stelzer, Frank Englert, Stephan Hörold, and Cindy Mayas. 2016. Improving service quality in public transportation systems using automated customer feedback. *Transportation Research Part E: Logistics and Transportation Review*, 89:259–271.

Jana Švárová. 2008. *Politeness markers in spoken language.* Ph.D. thesis, Masarykova univerzita, Pedagogická fakulta.

Hanna M Wallach. 2006. Topic modeling: beyond bag-of-words. In *Proceedings of the 23rd international conference on Machine learning*, pages 977–984. ACM.

Kohei Watanabe. 2018. Newsmap: A semi-supervised approach to geographical news classification. *Digital Journalism*, 6(3):294–309.

Theresa Wilson, Janyce Wiebe, and Paul Hoffmann. 2005. Recognizing contextual polarity in phrase-level sentiment analysis. In *Proceedings of Human Language Technology Conference and Conference on Empirical Methods in Natural Language Processing.*

Shuang Wu, Sravanthi Bondugula, Florian Luisier, Xiaodan Zhuang, and Pradeep Natarajan. 2014. Zero-shot event detection using multi-modal fusion of weakly supervised concepts. In *Proceedings of the IEEE Conference on Computer Vision and Pattern Recognition*, pages 2665–2672.

Wei Yang, Luchen Tan, Chunwei Lu, Anqi Cui, Han Li, Xi Chen, Kun Xiong, Muzi Wang, Ming Li, Jian Pei, et al. 2019. Detecting customer complaint escalation with recurrent neural networks and manually-engineered features. In *Proceedings of the 2019 Conference of the North American Chapter of the Association for Computational Linguistics: Human Language Technologies, Volume 2 (Industry Papers)*, pages 56–63.

Z. Yu, R. K. Wong, C. Chi, and F. Chen. 2015. A semi-supervised learning approach for microblog sentiment classification. In *2015 IEEE International Conference on Smart City/SocialCom/SustainCom (SmartCity)*, pages 339–344.

Dingwen Zhang, Junwei Han, Lu Jiang, Senmao Ye, and Xiaojun Chang. 2017. Revealing event saliency in unconstrained video collection. *IEEE Transactions on Image Processing*, 26(4):1746–1758.

Zhu Zhang. 2005. Mining inter-entity semantic relations using improved transductive learning. In *Second International Joint Conference on Natural Language Processing: Full Papers.*

Xin Zheng, Aixin Sun, Sibo Wang, and Jialong Han. 2017. Semi-supervised event-related tweet identification with dynamic keyword generation. In *Proceedings of the 2017 ACM on Conference on Information and Knowledge Management*, pages 1619–1628.

Bin Zou, Vasileios Lampos, Russell Gorton, and Ingemar J Cox. 2016. On infectious intestinal disease surveillance using social media content. In *Proceedings of the 6th International Conference on Digital Health Conference*, pages 157–161. ACM.

Item-based Collaborative Filtering with BERT

Yuyangzi Fu
eBay Inc.
yfuyu@ebay.com

Tian Wang
eBay Inc.
twang5@ebay.com

Abstract

In e-commerce, recommender systems have become an indispensable part of helping users explore the available inventory. In this work, we present a novel approach for item-based collaborative filtering, by leveraging BERT to understand items, and score relevancy between different items. Our proposed method could address problems that plague traditional recommender systems such as cold start, and "more of the same" recommended content. We conducted experiments on a large-scale real-world dataset with full cold-start scenario, and the proposed approach significantly outperforms the popular Bi-LSTM model.

1 Introduction

Recommender systems are an integral part of e-commerce platforms, helping users pick out items of interest from large inventories at scale. Traditional recommendation algorithms can be divided into two types: collaborative filtering-based (Schafer et al., 2007; Linden et al., 2003) and content-based (Lops et al., 2011; Pazzani and Billsus, 2007). However, these have their own limitations when applied directly to real-world e-commerce platforms. For example, traditional user-based collaborative filtering recommendation algorithms (see, e.g., Schafer et al., 2007) find the most similar users based on the seed user's rated items, and then recommend new items which other users rated highly. For item-based collaborative filtering (see, e.g., Linden et al., 2003), given a seed item, recommended items are chosen to have most similar user feedback. However, for highly active e-commerce platforms with large and constantly changing inventory, both approaches are severely impacted by data sparsity in the user-item interaction matrix.

Content-based recommendation algorithms calculate similarities in content between candidate items and seed items that the user has provided feedback for (which may be implicit e.g. clicking, or explicit e.g. rating), and then select the most similar items to recommend. Although less impacted by data sparsity, due to their reliance on content rather than behavior, they can struggle to provide novel recommendations which may activate the user's latent interests, a highly desirable quality for recommender systems (Castells et al., 2011).

Due to the recent success of neural networks in multiple AI domains (LeCun et al., 2015) and their superior modeling capacity, a number of research efforts have explored new recommendation algorithms based on Deep Learning (see, e.g., Barkan and Koenigstein, 2016; He et al., 2017; Hidasi et al., 2015; Covington et al., 2016).

In this paper, we propose a novel approach for item-based collaborative filtering, by leveraging the BERT model (Devlin et al., 2018) to understand item titles and model relevance between different items. We adapt the masked language modelling and next sentence prediction tasks from the natural language context to the e-commerce context. The contributions of this work are summarized as follows:

- Instead of relying on unique item identifier to aggregate history information, we only use item's title as content, along with token embeddings to solve the cold start problem, which is the main shortcoming of traditional recommendation algorithms.

- By training model with user behavior data, our model learns user's latent interests more than item similarities, while traditional recommendation algorithms and some pair-wise deep learning algorithms only provide similar items which users may have bought.

- We conduct experiments on a large-scale e-

54

Proceedings of the 3rd Workshop on e-Commerce and NLP (ECNLP 3), pages 54–58
Online, July 10, 2020. ©2020 Association for Computational Linguistics

commerce dataset, demonstrating the effectiveness of our approach and producing recommendation results with higher quality.

2 Item-based Collaborative Filtering with BERT

As mentioned earlier, for a dynamic e-commerce platform, items enter and leave the market continuously, resulting in an extremely sparse user-item interaction matrix. In addition to the challenge of long-tail recommendations, this also requires the recommender system to be continuously retrained and redeployed in order to accommodate newly listed items. To address these issues, in our proposed approach, instead of representing each item with a unique identifier, we choose to represent each item with its title tokens, which are further mapped to a continuous vector representation. By doing so, essentially two items with the same title would be treated as the same, and can aggregate user behaviors accordingly. For a newly listed item in the cold-start setting, the model can utilize the similarity of the item title to ones observed before to find relevant recommended items.

The goal of item-based collaborative filtering is to score the relevance between two items, and for a seed item, the top scored items would be recommended as a result. Our model is based on BERT (Devlin et al., 2018). Rather than the traditional RNN / CNN structure, BERT adopts *transformer encoder* as a language model, and use attention mechanism to calculate the relationship between input and output. The training of BERT model can be divided into two parts: *Masked Language Model* and *Next Sentence Prediction*. We re-purpose these tasks for the e-commerce context into *Masked Language Model on Item Titles*, and *Next Purchase Prediction*. Since the distribution of item title tokens differs drastically from words in natural language which the original BERT model is trained on, retraining the masked language model allows better understanding of item information for our use-case. Next Purchase Prediction can directly be used as the relevance scoring function for our item collaborative filtering task.

2.1 Model

Our model is based on the architecture of BERT_{base} (Devlin et al., 2018). The encoder of BERT_{base} contains 12 Transformer layers, with 768 hidden units, and 12 self-attention heads.

2.1.1 Next Purchase Prediction

The goal of this task is to predict the next item a user is going to purchase given the seed item he/she has just bought. We start with a pre-trained BERT_{base} model, and fine-tune it for our next purchase prediction task. We feed seed item as sentence A, and target item as sentence B. Both item titles are concatenated and truncated to have at most 128 tokens, including one [CLS] and two [SEP] tokens. For a seed item, its positive items are generated by collecting items purchased within the same user session, and the negative ones are randomly sampled. Given the positive item set I_p, and the negative item set I_n, the cross-entropy loss for next purchase prediction may be computed as

$$L_{np} = - \sum_{i_j \in I_p} \log p(i_j) - \sum_{i_j \in I_n} \log(1 - p(i_j)). \tag{1}$$

2.1.2 Masked Language Model

As the distribution of item title tokens is different from the natural language corpus used to train BERT_{base}, we further fine-tune the model for the masked language model (MLM) task as well. In the masked language model task, we follow the training schema outlined in Devlin et al. (2018) wherein 15% of the tokens in the title are chosen to be replaced by [MASK], random token, or left unchanged, with a probability of 80%, 10% and 10% respectively. Given the set of chosen tokens M, the corresponding loss for masked language model is

$$L_{lm} = - \sum_{m_i \in M} \log p(m_i). \tag{2}$$

The whole model is optimized against the joint loss $L_{lm} + L_{np}$.

2.1.3 Bi-LSTM Model (baseline)

As the evaluation is conducted on the dataset having a complete cold-start setting, for the sake of comparison, we build a baseline model consisting of a title token embedding layer with 768 dimensions, a bidirectional LSTM layer with 64 hidden units, and a 2-layer MLP with 128 and 32 hidden units respectively. For every pair of items, the two titles are concatenated into a sequence. After going through the embedding layer, the bidirectional LSTM reads through the entire sequence and generates a representation at the last timestep. The MLP layer with logistic function produces the estimated

Method	Prec @1	Prec @10	Recall @10	NDCG @10
Bi-LSTM	0.064	0.029	0.295	0.163
$BERT_{base}$ w/o MLM	0.263	0.057	0.572	0.408
$BERT_{base}$	0.555	0.079	0.791	0.669

Table 1: Result on ranking the item

probability score. The baseline model is trained using the same cross-entropy loss shown in Eq. 1.

2.2 Dataset

We train our models on an e-commerce website data. We collected 8,001,577 pairs of items, of which 33% are co-purchased (BIN event) within the same user session, while the rest are randomly sampled as negative samples. 99.9999% of entries of the item-item interaction matrix is empty. The sparsity of data forces the model to focus on *generalization* rather than *memorization*. The rationale would be further explained with the presence of the statistics of our dataset. Another 250,799 pairs of items are sampled in the same manner for use as a validation set, for conducting early stopping for training.

For testing, in order to mimic the cold-start scenario in the production system wherein traditional item-item collaborative filtering fails completely, we sampled 10,000 pairs of co-purchased items with the seed item not present in the training set. For each positive sample containing a seed item and a ground-truth co-purchased item, we paired the seed item with 999 random negative samples, and for testing, we use the trained model to rank the total of 1000 items given each seed item.

3 Results

The results of our evaluation are presented in Table. 1. We do not consider the traditional item-to-item collaborative filtering model (Linden et al., 2003) here since the evaluation is conducted assuming a complete cold-start setting, with all seed items unobserved in the training set, resulting in complete failure of such a model. Following the same reason, other approaches relying on unique item identifier (e.g. itemId) couldn't be considered either in our experiment. We believe its a practical experiment setting, as for a large-scale e-commerce platform, a massive amount of new items would be created every moment, and ignoring those items from the recommender system would be costly and inefficient.

We observe that the proposed BERT model greatly outperforms the LSTM-based model. When only fine-tuned for the Next Purchase Prediction task, our model exceeds the baseline by 310.9%, 96.6%, 93.9%, and 150.3% in precision@1, precision@10, recall@10, and NDCG@10 respectively. When fine tuning for the masked language model task is added, we see the metrics improved further by another 111.0%, 38.6%, 38.3%, and 64.0%.

From the experiment, the superiority of proposed BERT model for item-based collaborative filtering is clear. It is also clear that adapting the token distribution for the e-commerce context with masked language model within BERT is essential for achieving the best performance.

In order to visually examine the quality of recommendations, we present the recommended items for two different seed items in Table. 2. For the first seed item 'Marvel Spiderman T-shirt Small Black Tee Superhero Comic Book Character', most of the recommended items are T-shirts, paired with clothing accessories and tableware decoration, all having Marvel as the theme. For the second seed item 'Microsoft Surface Pro 4 12.3" Multi-Touch Tablet (Intel i5, 128GB) + Keyboard', the recommended items span a wide range of categories including tablets, digital memberships, electronic accessories, and computer hardware. From these two examples, we see that the proposed model appears to automatically find relevant selection criteria without manual specification, as well as make decisions between focusing on a specific category and catering to a wide range of inventory by learning from the data.

4 Summary

In this paper, we adapt the BERT model for the task of item-based recommendations. Instead of directly representing an item with a unique identifier, we use the item's title tokens as content, along with token embeddings, to address the cold start problem. We demonstrate the superiority of our model over a traditional neural network model in understanding item titles and learning relationships between items across vast inventory.

Acknowledgments

The authors would like to thank Sriganesh Madhvanath, Hua Yang, Xiaoyuan Wu, Alan Lu, Timothy Heath, and Kyunghyun Cho for their support and discussion, as well as anonymous reviewers for their helpful comments.

References

Oren Barkan and Noam Koenigstein. 2016. Item2vec: neural item embedding for collaborative filtering. In *2016 IEEE 26th International Workshop on Machine Learning for Signal Processing (MLSP)*, pages 1–6. IEEE.

P Castells, S Vargas, and J Wang. 2011. Novelty and diversity metrics for recommender systems: choice, discovery and relevance. In *International Workshop on Diversity in Document Retrieval (DDR 2011) at the 33rd European Conference on Information Retrieval (ECIR 2011)*.

Paul Covington, Jay Adams, and Emre Sargin. 2016. Deep neural networks for youtube recommendations. In *Proceedings of the 10th ACM conference on recommender systems*, pages 191–198. ACM.

Jacob Devlin, Ming-Wei Chang, Kenton Lee, and Kristina Toutanova. 2018. Bert: Pre-training of deep bidirectional transformers for language understanding. *arXiv preprint arXiv:1810.04805*.

Xiangnan He, Lizi Liao, Hanwang Zhang, Liqiang Nie, Xia Hu, and Tat-Seng Chua. 2017. Neural collaborative filtering. In *Proceedings of the 26th international conference on world wide web*, pages 173–182. International World Wide Web Conferences Steering Committee.

Balázs Hidasi, Alexandros Karatzoglou, Linas Baltrunas, and Domonkos Tikk. 2015. Session-based recommendations with recurrent neural networks. *arXiv preprint arXiv:1511.06939*.

Yann LeCun, Yoshua Bengio, and Geoffrey Hinton. 2015. Deep learning. *nature*, 521(7553):436–444.

Greg Linden, Brent Smith, and Jeremy York. 2003. Amazon. com recommendations: Item-to-item collaborative filtering. *IEEE Internet computing*, (1):76–80.

Pasquale Lops, Marco De Gemmis, and Giovanni Semeraro. 2011. Content-based recommender systems: State of the art and trends. In *Recommender systems handbook*, pages 73–105. Springer.

Michael J Pazzani and Daniel Billsus. 2007. Content-based recommendation systems. In *The adaptive web*, pages 325–341. Springer.

J Ben Schafer, Dan Frankowski, Jon Herlocker, and Shilad Sen. 2007. Collaborative filtering recommender systems. In *The adaptive web*, pages 291–324. Springer.

A   Appendix

Seed: Marvel Spiderman T-shirt Small Black Tee Superhero Comic Book Character

Title	Score
Marvel Black Panther Character Men's Superhero Socks Black	0.9999
Marvel SPIDERMAN HOMECOMING Birthday Party Range Tableware Supplies Decorations	0.9999
Marvel Compression Leggings Superhero T-shirts Long Pants Spiderman Sportswear	0.9999
Venom T-Shirt Funny Baby Venom Spiderman Black T-Shirt for Men and Women	0.9998
SPIDERMAN HOMECOMING LOGO T-SHIRT	0.9998
Marvel Comics Books Avengers The Incredible Hulk Transforming Tee Shirt Black	0.9998
Mens Short Sleeve T Shirt Slim Fit Casual Tops Tee Batman Iron Man Spider-Man	0.9998
MEMORIES Stan Lee Marvel Superhero T-Shirt Artwork Spiderman Avengers Mens Top	0.9998
Marvel Spider-Man Superior Spider-Man Mens Black T-Shirt	0.9998
Marvel Spider-Man: Far From Home Red Glow Mens Graphic T Shirt	0.9998

Seed: Microsoft Surface Pro 4 12.3" Multi-Touch Tablet (Intel i5, 128GB) + Keyboard

Title	Score
Microsoft Surface 2 1573 ARM Cortex-A15 1.7GHz 2GB 64GB SSD 10.8" Touch	0.9998
Microsoft Xbox Live 3 Month Gold Membership Instant Delivery, Retail $24.99	0.9998
Genuine OEM 1625 AC Power Charger Adapter For Microsoft Surface Pro 3	0.9997
For Sale Microsoft Surface Pro LCD display Touch Screen Digitizer Glass Assembly	0.9997
65W AC Adapter For Microsoft Surface Book/ Pro 4 Q4Q-00001 1706 15V 4A	0.9997
4GB 8GB 16GB DDR3 1333 MHz PC3-10600 DIMM 240Pin Desktop Memory Ram	0.9995
Samsung Galaxy Tab A 10.1" Tablet 16GB Android OS - Black (SM-T580NZKAXAR)	0.9994
For Microsoft Surface Pro 4 1724 Touch Screen LCD Flex Cable Ribbon X937072-001	0.9993
RSIM 12+ 2018 R-SIM Nano Unlock Card Fits for iPhone XS MAX/XR/X/8/	0.9993
Intel Core i5-4570S Quad-Core Socket LGA1150 CPU Processor SR14J 2.90GHz	0.9993

Table 2: Sample recommended items with seeds

Semi-supervised Category-specific Review Tagging on Indonesian E-Commerce Product Reviews

Meng Sun
Tokopedia, Singapore
daisy.meng@tokopedia.com

Marie Stephen Leo
Tokopedia, Singapore
marie.leo@tokopedia.com

Eram Munawwar
Tokopedia, Singapore
eram.munawwar@tokopedia.com

Seong Per Lee
Tokopedia, Singapore
seong.lee@tokopedia.com

Albert Hidayat
Tokopedia, Jakarta
albert.hidayat@tokopedia.com

Muhamad Danang Kerianto
Tokopedia, Jakarta

Paul C. Condylis
Tokopedia, Singapore
paul.condylis@tokopedia.com

Sheng-yi Kong
Tokopedia, Singapore
angus.kong@tokopedia.com

Abstract

Product reviews are a huge source of natural language data in e-commerce applications. Several millions of customers write reviews regarding a variety of topics. We categorize these topics into two groups as either "category-specific" topics or as "generic" topics that span multiple product categories. While we can use a supervised learning approach to tag review text for generic topics, it is impossible to use supervised approaches to tag category-specific topics due to the sheer number of possible topics for each category. In this paper, we present an approach to tag each review with several product category-specific tags on Indonesian language product reviews using a semi-supervised approach. We show that our proposed method can work at scale on real product reviews at Tokopedia[1], a major e-commerce platform in Indonesia. Manual evaluation shows that the proposed method can efficiently generate category-specific product tags.

1 Introduction

E-commerce product reviews are a rich source of direct feedback from the customers. Written in free text natural language, product reviews contain a significant amount of information regarding a variety of topics that are important to prospective buyers.

Tokopedia conducted customer survey research to understand the sources of information that potential buyers assess while making a purchase decision. This internal research shows that around 15% customers consider product reviews as the most important source of information and it is the third highest among all 20 possible information sources. Internal analysis of the "click rate" of various components on the platform's product listing page also shows that components related to product reviews have the second highest click rate which further emphasises the importance of product reviews for prospective buyers.

Although reviews are important information sources, manually filtering relevant information is a cumbersome process for a buyer when making a purchase decision. Tokopedia has several hundreds of millions of customer reviews, generated by millions of users over the years. Therefore, extracting relevant tags for each product so that prospective buyers can quickly filter the most relevant reviews based on their topic of interest becomes important to make a quick purchase decision and improve buyer engagement on the platform.

We categorize topics in reviews into two types. The first type of topics are the generic topics that exist in reviews of products from any category, and they are about the generic information that customers care about. In the e-commerce platform, for example, the generic topics are "customer service", "delivery, "packaging quality", "price", and so on. The second type of topics are the category-specific topics. These topics are detailed description of the product specific attributes. Since different products have different attributes, the category-specific topics are very different for products from different categories. For example, for products in Phone Case category, the category-specific topic could be "cable hole", while for products in Herbal Medicine category, the category-specific topic would be "ingredients". The focus of this paper is to generate tags of category-specific topics for products across different categories.

---

[1] `www.tokopedia.com`

59

Proceedings of the 3rd Workshop on e-Commerce and NLP (ECNLP 3), pages 59–63
Online, July 10, 2020. ©2020 Association for Computational Linguistics

There are several challenges for this work. Firstly, the category-specific topics are widely different among products of different categories. Therefore, it's impossible to get labeled data to apply supervised methods which are normally used when generating tags. Secondly, we work on informal Indonesian language. Though Indonesian language shares the same alphabet with English, Indonesian language differs from English in certain significant ways such as different sentence structure, prefix and suffix modifiers and slang spellings. Also since we work on reviews, the texts are informal, and contain a mixture of Indonesian, English, abbreviations and slang, which further increases the difficulty.

The focus of this work is to address the above mentioned challenges. We proposed a semi-supervised method, and successfully applied it to product reviews from different categories in the e-commerce platform. We also evaluated our results with manually labeled data.

The rest of this paper is organized as follows. We describe related work in the literature in Section 2. We then describe our approach to extract category-specific tags from Indonesian language review text in Section 3. Experiments and results are discussed in Section 4.

2 Related Work

While we can use a supervised learning approach to get generic topics from product reviews, it is impossible to use supervised approaches with "category-specific" topics due to the sheer number of possible topics for each product category. Therefore, we use an unsupervised method to extract topics from product reviews in this paper.

One of the earliest unsupervised method to extract keywords from text is the statistics based method. Frequency or Term Frequency - Inverse Document Frequency (TF-IDF) score is calculated on the n-grams of all the reviews. The n-grams with higher score will be extracted as tags. Graph-based methods (Mihalcea and Tarau, 2004; Altuncu et al., 2019) can also used to extract keywords, where each token is a vertex and an edge is defined when two tokens are in the same context window. Both methods however, fail to group n-grams of similar meaning together.

Latent Dirichlet Allocation (LDA) (Blei et al., 2003) and it's variants (Yan et al., 2013; Xiong and Guo, 2019) are popular methods to group words into topics. However LDA processes a document as a bag of words with the assumption that each word is independent of each other. Therefore this method loses valuable occurrence information. Clustering method like k-means, DBSCAN can group similar words based on word embedding. However, word embedding is high dimensional data and clustering fails to work well on it due to the curse of dimensionality.

A neural network model was proposed by He et al. (2017) to group phrases into topics. It overcomes the drawbacks of LDA and clustering methods by utilizing the embedding information with attention mechanism to attend to important tokens in the sentence. We use this model in this paper.

3 Category-specific Tag Generation Approach

In this section we describe how the category-specific topic and the product tags are generated. The pipeline is shown in Figure. 1.

3.1 Phrase Extraction

We extract phrases from each text review using Stanford NLP's dependency parser (Manning et al., 2014). Among all the extracted dependencies (Nivre et al., 2016), we choose three kinds as shown in Table 1. These dependencies are about nouns, as the phrases extracted by them are more likely to be about the products. Examples of dependencies that are not selected such as verb, adverb and so on is shown in Table 2.

UDP	meaning	example
amod	adjectival modifier	Sam eats red meat
nsubj	nominal subject	The car is red .
compound	compound	Phone book

Table 1: Universal Dependency Relations (UDP) chosen to extract phrases from product reviews. (`https://universaldependencies.org/u/dep/`) (We show examples in English.)

We further drop phrases which contain stop words derived from NLTK Indonesian stop word list (`https://www.nltk.org/`), and a list that is manually labeled by an internal product team. We only remove stopwords after phrase extraction, since phrase extraction needs the complete sentence input to extract phrases more accurately.

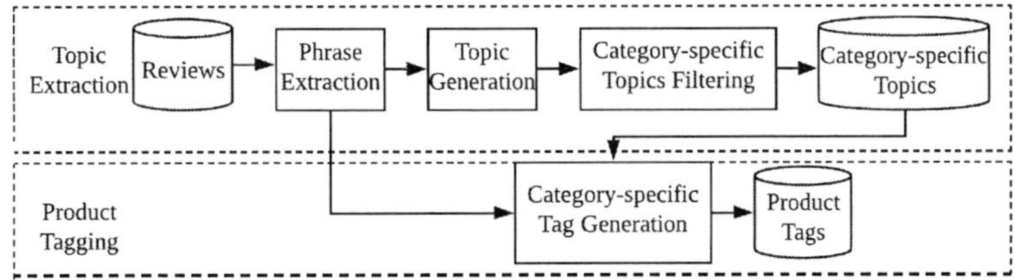

Figure 1: Category-specific topic extraction and product tagging pipelines

UDP	meaning	example
advmod	adverb modifier	less often
obj	object	She gave me a raise
csubj	casual object	What she said is interesting

Table 2: Examples of the dependencies not selected for phrase extraction. (We show examples in English.)

3.2 Topic Generation

A topic is a group of phrases sharing a similar concept. Different topics, on the other hand, are separate groups of phrases of different concepts. On the phrases from each product category, we apply the Unsupervised Aspect Extraction (UAE) model (He et al., 2017) to extract topics. The UAE model generates topics by first learning K topic embeddings, the number of topics K is predefined. Phrases within a product category are then grouped to the topic that is closest in embedding.

As shown in Figure 2, the model has three layers: the embedding layer, the attention layer and the auto-encoder layer. We concatenate the review

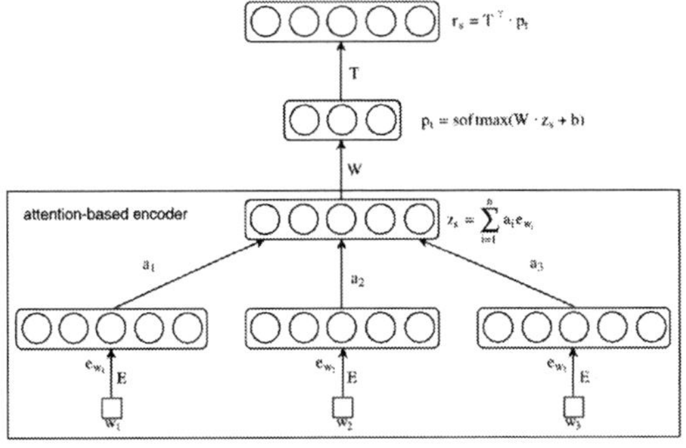

Figure 2: UAE Model Structure

phrases from one product as the input to the embedding layer. The embedding layer is initialized with a word2vec embedding of dimension d, that is trained on all the reviews of this category. Since

StanfordNLP dependency parser generates phrases with two tokens, concatenating the embeddings of each token in the phrase gives us a phrase embedding of dimension $2d$.

The attention layer takes these phrase embeddings, and calculates a weighted sum of the phrases, as $\mathbf{z}_s = \sum_{i=1}^{n} a_i \mathbf{e}_{w_i}$, where $\mathbf{e}_{w_i} \in \mathbb{R}^{1 \times 2d}$ is the embedding for the ith input phrase, and a_i is the weight computed by the attention layer based on both the relevance of the filtered phrase to the K aspects and the relevance to the whole sentence which is trained with the following formulas.

$$a_i = \frac{\exp(d_i)}{\sum_{j=1}^{n} \exp(d_j)}$$

$$d_i = \mathbf{e}_{w_i}^T \cdot \mathbf{M} \cdot \mathbf{y}_s$$

$$\mathbf{y}_s = \frac{1}{n} \sum_{i=1}^{n} \mathbf{e}_{w_i}$$

In the auto-encoder layer, the encoder compresses $\mathbf{z}_s$ to a vector of probabilities $\mathbf{p}_t$ with $\mathbf{p}_t = \text{softmax}(\mathbf{W} \cdot \mathbf{z}_s + \mathbf{b})$ and the decoder reconstructs a sentence embedding with $\mathbf{r}_s = \mathbf{T}^T \cdot \mathbf{p}_t$. Here $\mathbf{T} \in \mathbb{R}^{K \cdot 2d}$ is the learned aspect embedding matrix, which is in the same embedding space as the phrase embedding.

The loss function of the model is defined as $L(\theta) = J(\theta) + \lambda U(\theta)$, where θ represents the model parameter, $J(\theta)$ is proportional to the hinge loss between $\mathbf{r}_s$ and $\mathbf{z}_s$, and $U(\theta)$ is the regularization term which encourages orthogonality among the rows in the aspect embedding T.

3.3 Category-specific Topic Filtering

Category-specific topics are unique to each product category and not generic. To sift out the general topics from all the generated topics, we use a supervised method.

As the generic topics are similar across all product categories, we made a general word list which contains the frequent words in general phrases. Examples from the general word list are *berfungsi,*

semoga, bonus, sis, kwalitas, oke, super, boss.
(The English translations are *function, hopefully, bonuses, sis, quality, okay, super, boss.*)

A phrase is considered a general phrase if both words in the phrase are in the general word list. If more than a certain percentage η of all the phrases in one topic are general phrases, the topic is considered a general topic, otherwise the topic is a generated category-specific topic, which will be used in the next step.

After supervised filtering, manual labeling is applied to each phrase on the generated category-specific topics. Since we've already applied topic extraction and supervised filtering, the number of phrases to be manually labeled is reduced dramatically. For each phrase, we label it either as generic, incoherent or category-specific. Generic phrases are those phrases about general aspects, including delivery, fits description, packing quality, customer service, price. General descriptions about the product quality are also general phrases, these phrases can be used to describe products from most of other categories as well, such as *produk bagus (good product)*. Incoherent phrases are those that are not about the same concept as the majority of the other phrases in the same topic. And category-specific phrases are the phrase about the category-specific aspects of the category, and they are coherent with the majority of the phrases in the same topic.

The category-specific phrases in each topic will be used for tag generation as will be described in Section 3.4. And the frequent words in the generic phrases will be added to the general word list for use in supervised filtering of future topics.

3.4 Category-specific Tag Generation

With the filtered category-specific topics, we generate the category-specific tags.

For each product, we group the review phrases to corresponding topics as discussed in Section 3.1 and Section 3.2. We use supervised method shown in Section 3.3 to filter category-specific topics from all the generated topics. Then, we rank the phrases in each topic according to the frequency of phrases in the reviews of this product and choose the one with highest ranking as the tag of this topic for this product. The results are uploaded to a data warehouse.

4 Experimental Setup

In this section, we apply our proposed method to product reviews from Tokopedia. We demonstrate the experimental results, and show the evaluation results of the generated category-specific topics.

4.1 Data

We use reviews from 89.5 Million products across 18 product categories as the dataset. The average number of reviews in each category, and the average string length of reviews in shown in Table 3 (column: "#reviews" and "average length").

Category English	# reviews	Average length	# topics	average p@100	topic rate
Handphone Charger	518890	58.03	5	69	100%
Men Sneakers	474767	55.28	3	63	50%
Men Analogue Clock	461819	58.96	5	64	83%
Plant seeds	309374	58.47	7	78	88%

Table 3: Product review statistics and evaluation results for 4 sample categories.

4.2 Model Result

After doing phrase extraction, we applied UAE model for topic extraction. We performed the same preprocessing as He et al. (2017) and used word2vec to train the word embeddings with dimension $d = 200$. We modified the model structure to accept phrase input as described in Section 3.2, and we shared the same parameter settings as He et al. (2017). We apply our method to each category separately, and we set the number of topics as $K = 14$ for topic generation. Then, we apply category-specific filter on the extracted topics for all categories with $\eta = 40\%$. The general word list we used contains 127 words.

The average time to get generated category-specific topics on extracted phrases is 2 hours per category with around 0.5M reviews. On average, we generate 5 category-specific topics for each category. We show the number of generated category-specific topics for each category in Table 3 (column: "#topics"). We show some of these generated category-specific topics in Table 4.

4.3 Evaluation

The most essential part of this work is the automatic generation of category-specific topics. In this section, we show the evaluation results for the quality of the category-specific topic generation.

Category English		Topic Example
Handphone	Id	android hp,sony hp,lenovo hp,mini ipad
Charger	En	android hp,sony hp,lenovo hp,mini ipad
Men	Id	sesuai model,sesuai size,sesuai bentuk
Sneakers	En	fit models, fit sizes, fit shapes
Men Analogue	Id	automatic jam, pria jam,jutaan jamm
Clock	En	automatic clocks,men clocks,millions of hours
Plant Seeds	Id	semi tumbuh,bismillah tumbuh,daya tumbuh
	En	spring grows, bismillah grows, power grows

Table 4: Example of generated category-specific topics in Indonesian language (Id) for four selected categories and their English (En) translations.

4.3.1 Evaluation Metric

An internal product team labeled the results from supervised filtering. They label each phrase as category-specific, general or incoherent as described in Section 3.3. On average, it took one person 3 minutes to label all the phrases of one topic. We apply the evaluation metrics used in He et al. (2017) and Chen et al. (2014). Following their setting, we get the score $precision@n$ ($p@n$) for each generated category-specific topic, as the number of category-specific phrases among the top n phrases. We show the average $p@100$ for sample categories in Table 3 (column: "average $p@100$"). From the result, we can see the majority of the phrases in the generated topics are category-specific in meaning.

We define any topic with $p@n > 60$ as a category-specific topic, and we define topic rate as

$$\text{topic rate} = \frac{\#\text{category-specific topics}}{\#\text{generated category-specific topics}}$$

We show the topic rate for selected category in Table 3 (column: "topic rate"). We can see more than half of the generated category-specific topics will be selected after manual filtering, thus, human labeling will be very efficient on the automatically generated category-specific topics.

5 Conclusion

In this paper, we described a pipeline for category-specific review tagging using phrase extraction, topic generation, category-specific topic filtering and tag generation. Given the product reviews, the pipeline generates the category-specific tags for each product and customers can filter product reviews with these tags. The pipeline is being implemented on product reviews at Tokopedia, and proved to be successful when scaled to large number of reviews. We also evaluated the quality of the generated category-specific topics with manual labeling and results show that the pipeline can generate coherent category-specific topics.

References

M Tarik Altuncu, Eloise Sorin, Joshua D Symons, Erik Mayer, Sophia N Yaliraki, Francesca Toni, and Mauricio Barahona. 2019. Extracting information from free text through unsupervised graph-based clustering: an application to patient incident records. *arXiv preprint arXiv:1909.00183.*

David M. Blei, Andrew Y. Ng, and Michael I. Jordan. 2003. Latent dirichlet allocation. *Journal of Machine Learning Research*, 3:993–1022.

Zhiyuan Chen, Arjun Mukherjee, and Bing Liu. 2014. Aspect extraction with automated prior knowledge learning. In *Proceedings of the 52nd Annual Meeting of the Association for Computational Linguistics (Volume 1: Long Papers)*, pages 347–358, Baltimore, Maryland.

Ruidan He, Wee Sun Lee, Hwee Tou Ng, and Daniel Dahlmeier. 2017. An unsupervised neural attention model for aspect extraction. In *Proceedings of the 55th Annual Meeting of the Association for Computational Linguistics*, pages 388–397, Vancouver, Canada.

Christopher D. Manning, Mihai Surdeanu, John Bauer, Jenny Finkel, Steven J. Bethard, and David McClosky. 2014. The Stanford CoreNLP natural language processing toolkit. In *Association for Computational Linguistics (ACL) System Demonstrations*, pages 55–60.

Rada Mihalcea and Paul Tarau. 2004. Textrank: Bringing order into text. In *Proceedings of the 2004 Conference on Empirical Methods in Natural Language Processing*, pages 404–411, Barcelona, Spain.

Joakim Nivre, Marie-Catherine De Marneffe, Filip Ginter, Yoav Goldberg, Jan Hajic, Christopher D Manning, Ryan McDonald, Slav Petrov, Sampo Pyysalo, Natalia Silveira, et al. 2016. Universal dependencies v1: A multilingual treebank collection. In *Proceedings of the 10th International Conference on Language Resources and Evaluation (LREC'16)*, pages 1659–1666.

Ao Xiong and Qing Guo. 2019. Chinese news keyword extraction algorithm based on textrank and topic model. In *International Conference on Artificial Intelligence for Communications and Networks*, pages 334–341. Springer.

Xiaohui Yan, Jiafeng Guo, Yanyan Lan, and Xueqi Cheng. 2013. A biterm topic model for short texts. In *Proceedings of the 22nd International Conference on World Wide Web*, pages 1445–1456, Rio de Janeiro, Brazil.

Deep Hierarchical Classification for Category Prediction in E-commerce System

Dehong Gao, Wenjing Yang, Huiling Zhou, Yi Wei, Yi Hu and Hao Wang
Alibaba Group
Hangzhou City, Zhejiang Province, China
{dehong.gdh, carrie.ywj, zhule.zhl, yi.weiy, erwin.huy, longran.wh}@alibaba-inc.com

Abstract

In e-commerce system, category prediction is to automatically predict categories of given texts. Different from traditional classification where there are no relations between classes, category prediction is reckoned as a standard hierarchical classification problem since categories are usually organized as a hierarchical tree. In this paper, we address hierarchical category prediction. We propose a Deep Hierarchical Classification framework, which incorporates the multi-scale hierarchical information in neural networks and introduces a representation sharing strategy according to the category tree. We also define a novel combined loss function to punish hierarchical prediction losses. The evaluation shows that the proposed approach outperforms existing approaches in accuracy.

1 Introduction

Category Prediction (CP), which aims to recognize the intent categories of given texts, is regarded as one of the most fundamental machine learning tasks in e-commerce system (Ali et al., 2016). For example, this predicted category information will influence product ranking in search and recommendation system.

Different from the traditional classification (Yann et al., 1998; Larkey and Croft, 1996) CP is formally categorized as a hierarchical classification task since categories in most e-commerce websites are organized as a hierarchical tree (we consider the situation that the categories are organized as a hierarchical tree, but not a directed acyclic graph). Figure 1.(a) shows a simplified fragment of one category architecture. Apart from CP, there are also many other tasks belonging to hierarchical classification, e.g., image classification shown in Figure 1.(b).

For simplicity, most practical approaches ignore the relation information between classes (hereafter referred to as flat classification). These approaches are easily implemented, but disadvantage in accuracy (Rohit et al., 2013). In academy, the hierarchical classification problem is not well-studied as well (Silla and Freitas., 2011). Except these flat approaches, published studies are mainly divided into two directions: the local approaches, and the global approaches (Carlos and Freitas., 2009). The local approaches learn multiple independent classifiers, each classifier either for per node, or for per parent node or for per layer. Taking the local approach for per layer as an example, for Figure 1.(b) it will train two independent classifiers for layer_1 and layer_leaf, respectively. The global approaches regard all none-root nodes as the classes to predict. Only one classifier is trained for all these none-root classes. We argue that all these approaches either do not consider the hierarchical structure at all (i.e., the flat approaches), or take implicit or tiny consideration of the class hierarchy.

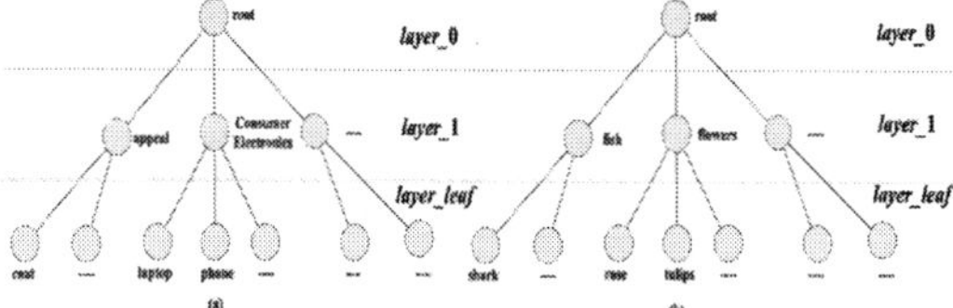

Figure 1. Hierarchical Classification Tasks

The main challenges in hierarchical classification are at two aspects: hierarchical representation in classification model and hierarchical inconsistency in training process. Hierarchical representation means researchers may select Naive Bayesian (Larkey and Croft, 1996), Support Vector Machine (Chang and Lin, 2009), and Neural Networks (Jurgen Schmidhuber, 2015) as their classification models. But the hierarchical information fails to be explicitly incorporated in these models. Consequentially, it is hard for these models to learn the complex hierarchical information. The hierarchical inconsistency means

Proceedings of the 3rd Workshop on e-Commerce and NLP (ECNLP 3), pages 64–68
Online, July 10, 2020. ©2020 Association for Computational Linguistics

if a text is predicted as "appeal" in the layer_1, but as "laptop" in the leaf layer during training phase in Figure 1.(a), none approach can deal with this inconsistency as far as we known.

To solve these two problems, we propose a general Deep Hierarchical Classification (DHC) framework. Firstly, according to hierarchical representation, our DHC approach directly incorporates class hierarchy information in neural network. DHC first generates one hierarchical layer representation for per layer. Inspired by the idea that sibling classes under one parent class must share certain common information, we introduce a hierarchical representation sharing strategy that the representation of one lower layer should include the representation information about its upper layer. This sharing strategy is recursively carried on in a top-down manner according to the class hierarchy. As a result, the classification model is forced to learn this structure information, and the class hierarchy information is "explicitly" involved in the model. Secondly, according to hierarchical inconsistency, we define a hierarchical loss function composed of the layer loss and the dependence loss. The layer loss defines the training loss within layers, which is the same to the loss in traditional flat classification. The proposed dependence loss defines the loss between layers. When predictions of two successive layers are inconsistent (i.e., these two predicted classes are not in a parent-child relationship), we will add an additional dependence loss to compel the classification model to learn this relation information. The dependence loss function is hierarchy-related and is regarded as a punishment when predictions are not consistent with the category structure. By this way, we can deal with the hierarchical inconsistency during the training process.

DHC can be regarded as a general hierarchical classification framework, we evaluate it with text and image classification. For text classification, we collect query-category and title-category pairs from one e-commence website. For image classification we adopt the commonly-used cifar100 dataset. Taking advantage of hierarchical representation and hierarchical loss function, the DHC approach significantly improves the accuracy. Our main contributions include the novel DHC framework and the hierarchical representation and hierarchical loss which are first proposed as far as we know. All of them will be detailed in the following sections.

2 Deep Hierarchical Classification

Mathematically, the hierarchical classification task can be formulated as: *Given*:

Input X: X can denote the text or the image inputs.

Category tree $\mathcal{T}$: Categories are organized by a category tree $\mathcal{T}$ with L hierarchical layers. The categories (i.e., classes to predict) are denoted by Y. Categories of different layers are dependent as $Y_L \Rightarrow Y_{L-1} \Rightarrow \cdots \Rightarrow Y_1$ ($\Rightarrow$ denotes the IS-A relation in category tree $\mathcal{T}$.)

Output: **Categories of input** X: Predict categories of the given input X. Since categories are hierarchically related, it is possible to predict the leaf class and infer the classes of all the other layers according to category tree $\mathcal{T}$.

In the DHC approach, we defines a neural network model $\mathcal{N}(\theta)$ where θ are the parameters to be estimated. Taking a three-layer hierarchical classification problem as an example, we show the DHC neural network in Figure 2. The neural network is composed of three parts: **Flat Neural Network (FNN), Hierarchical Embedding Network (HEN)** and **Hierarchical Loss Network (HLN)**. We will further discuss these three parts.

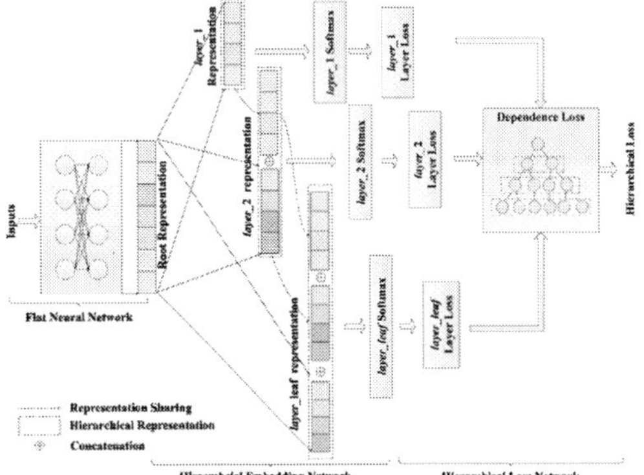

Figure 2. Deep Hierarchical Classification (Take three-layer hierarchical classification as example)

2.1 Flat Neural Network

Given an input X, FNN is used to generate a root representation. For our main contributions lay in the HEN and HLN, we can adopt a state-of-the-art neural network in practice. Let $\mathcal{N}_{flat}(\theta_{flat})$ denote this flat neural network, the output is viewed as the root representation R_0

$$R_0 = \mathcal{N}_{flat}(X, \theta_{flat}) \qquad (1)$$

2.2 Hierarchical Embedding Network

With the root representation, HEN aims to produce hierarchical representations for every layers. For the lth layer, we first produce the independent representation R_l', i.e.,

$$R_l' = W_{r_l} * R_0 \tag{2}$$

where W_{r_l} represents the weights for the independent layer representation. The independent layer representation is hierarchical-free. As mentioned, classes belonging to the same parent class share certain common information. The representation of one lower layer should include the representation information about its upper layer. Thus, the hierarchical representation R_l is computed by concatenating the independent representations of all previous layers denoting by

$$\begin{aligned} R_l &= R_{l-1} \oplus R_l' \quad for\ l \neq 1 \\ R_l &= R_l' \quad\quad\quad for\ l = 1 \end{aligned} \tag{3}$$

For the lth layer prediction, the hierarchical representation R_l is passed into a softmax regression layer. The output of the softmax regression layer is denoted by

$$\tilde{y}_{li} = \frac{e^{W_{s_{li}} R_l}}{\sum_{k=1}^{|l|} e^{W_{s_{lk}} R_l}} \tag{4}$$

where W_{s_l} are the parameters of the lth softmax regression layer. $\tilde{y}_{li}$ denotes the prediction probability of the ith class in the lth hierarchy layer. $|l|$ denotes the number of classes in the lth hierarchy layer.

2.3 Hierarchical Loss Network

According to hierarchical layer representations and document true classes, HLN will compute the hierarchical loss to estimate the neural network parameters. We propose two types of losses, i.e., the layer loss and the dependency loss. Concretely, the lth layer loss function $lloss_l$ is defined as

$$lloss_l = -\sum_{j=0}^{|l|} y_{lj} \log(\tilde{y}_{lj}) \tag{5}$$

y_{lj} is the expected output of the jth class in the lth hierarchy layer. To measure the prediction errors between layers, we propose a dependence loss. If the predicted classes of two successive layers are not parent-child relation, a dependence loss appears to punish the learning model for it does not predict the classes according to the hierarchy

structure. The lth layer dependence loss $dloss_l$ is defined as

$$dloss_l = -\left(ploss_{(l-1)}\right)^{\mathbb{D}_l \mathbb{I}_{l-1}} (ploss_l)^{\mathbb{D}_l \mathbb{I}_l} \tag{6}$$

where $\mathbb{D}_l$ and $\mathbb{I}_l$ denote that whether the model predictions conflict category structure, especially

$$\begin{aligned} \mathbb{D}_l &= \begin{cases} 1 & if\ \hat{y}_l \nrightarrow \hat{y}_{l-1} \\ 0 & else \end{cases} \\ \mathbb{I}_l &= \begin{cases} 1 & if\ \hat{y}_l \neq y_l \\ 0 & else \end{cases} \end{aligned} \tag{7}$$

Here $\hat{y}_l = \max_i \tilde{y}_{li}$ denotes the predicted class, and y_l is the true label of the query. $\mathbb{D}_l$ denotes whether the predicted label in the lth layer is a child class of the predicted class in the $l-1^{\text{th}}$ layer. $\mathbb{I}_l$ denotes whether the lth layer prediction is correct. $ploss_l$ is a dependence punishment to force the neural network to learn structure information from the category structure. $ploss_l$ can be set as a constant or related to the prediction error.

Finally, the total loss is defined as the weighted summation of the layer losses and the dependence losses, i.e.,

$$J(\theta) = \sum_{i=1}^{L} \alpha_i lloss_i + \sum_{i=2}^{L} \beta_i dloss_i \tag{8}$$

where α and β $(0 \leq \alpha, \beta \leq 1)$ are the loss weights of different layers.

In the inference phase, there are mainly three methods to determine the category of one text, the heuristic method, the greedy method and the beam search method (Wu et al., 2016). We adopt the greedy method in our experiments for fair comparison.

Datasets	Sample	1st&2nd layer
Query-Category	1.3millions	39/742
Title-Category	30.7millions	39/742
Cifar100[1]	60thousands	20/100

Table 1. Information of experiment datasets

3 Experiments

3.1 Datasets

As DHC is a general hierarchical classification framework, we experiment on text classification and image classification with both industry and public datasets, respectively. For text classification, we collect two datasets, i.e., <Query-Category> (user query and the category of one user-clicked product) and <Title-Category> (product title and its category). For image classification, we experiment on the cifar100 dataset, in which the

---

1 https://www.cs.toronto.edu/~kriz/cifar.html

fine and coarse labels are organized by a three-layer hierarchical tree. The information of these three datasets (e.g., sample numbers and class numbers) are shown in Table 1.

For text classification, query-category and title-category corpus are randomly divided into ten equal parts. Nine parts are used in the training phase and the other one is used in the test phase. For image classification, we use the official training/testing parts. Accuracy is selected to evaluate the performances (Kiritchenko and Stan, 2005; Kiritchenko and Stan, 2006).

Accuracy	Query-Category		Title-Category	
	1st layer	2nd layer	1st layer	2nd layer
SVM	88.1%	67.99%	85.34%	60.13%
HSVM	89.98%	68.59%	88.14%	63.59%
FastText	90.10%	67.64%	88.06%	61.62%
TextCNN	90.11%	68.29%	89.10%	64.31%
HiNet	91.54%	72.98%	90.69%	65.10%
DHC	**92.10%**	**73.37%**	**91.21%**	**69.02%**

Table 2. Accuracy evaluation of SVM, HSVM, FastText, TextCNN, HiNet and DHC approaches for text classification

Accuracy	Cifar100	
	1st layer	2nd layer
KerasCNN	89.23%	67.89%
HiNet	90.11%	72.23%
DHC	**92.21%**	**75.91%**

Table 3. Accuracy evaluation of baseline, HiNet and DHC approaches for image classification

3.2 Evaluation of baseline and existing approaches

In this set of experiments, we compare our approach with the existing approaches.

For text classification, SVM (Chang and Lin, 2009), FastText (Joulin et al., 2016), and TextCNN (Yoon Kim, 2014) are selected as the flat baselines and we train two classifiers for the two layers, respectively. HSVM (Tsochantaridis et al., 2005) and HiNet (Wu and Saito, 2017) are selected as hierarchical baselines. For fair competition, HiNet and DHC are adopted the same network architecture with TextCNN as the base model. The purpose is to verify the effectiveness of our DHC framework, but not the based model.

With the limited space, the standard neural network (KerasCNN)[2] and HiNET are adopted as the flat and hierarchical baselines in image classification, respectively. HiNET and DHC keep the same network architecture and hyper-parameters with KerasCNN. We also focus on the comparison of the DHC framework, rather than the base model.

The accuracies of these four approaches are shown in Table 2 and Table 3, which shows that DHC outperforms all the other approaches. The layer representation sharing and hierarchical loss computation help the improvement in performance. Meanwhile, we find that the accuracy increase of the leaf layer is greater than that of the layer_1. This is because the classification for the layer_1 is much easier than that for the leaf layer. The classifiers can learn comparable models for the layer_1, but DHC shows its powerful ability in the leaf layer classification.

3.3 Evaluation of HEN and HLN

This set of experiments is to reveal the influence of HEN and HLN. HiNet is adopted as the baseline approach and the experiments are conducted on title-category dataset for simplicity.

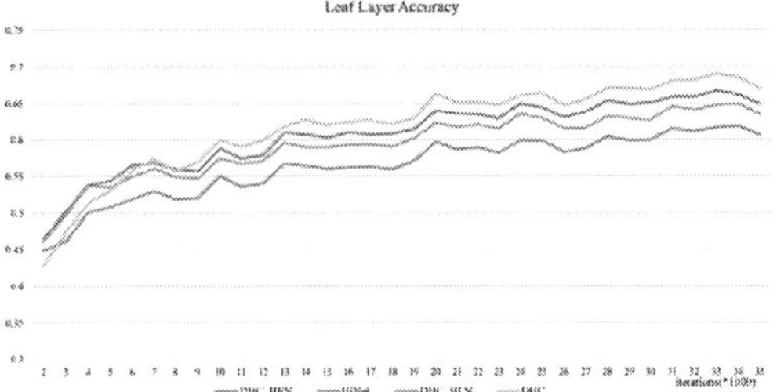

Figure 3. Accuracy evaluation of HiNet, DHC_HEN ($\beta = 0$ in Equation 8), DHC_HLN ($R_l = R_l'$ in Equation 3) and DHC approaches

Figure 3 illustrates the accuracy changes of the leaf layer prediction in the training iteration. Compared to HiNet, it indicates that both HEN and HLN have the positive influence for hierarchical classification. HEN contributes more than HLN. We find that the definition of the hierarchical loss function affects the robustness and accuracy of the classification a lot. A proper hierarchical loss function definition is still an open question.

4 Conclusions

In sum, we extensively address the two challenges (i.e., hierarchical representation and hierarchical inconsistency) in hierarchical classification and propose the DHC approach to solve these two problems. Experiments both on text and image

---

2 https://keras.io/examples/cifar10_cnn/

classification demonstrate the effectiveness of our proposed DHC approach.

References

Cevahir Ali and Murakami Koji. 2016. Large-scale Multi-class and Hierarchical Product Categorization for an E-commerce Giant. In *Proceedings of the 26th International Conference on Computational Linguistics*: Technical Papers 22(1): 525-535.

Silla Jr. Carlos and Alex A Freitas. 2009. A Global-Model Naive Bayes Approach to the Hierarchical Prediction of Protein Functions. In *Proceedings of the 2009 Ninth IEEE International Conference on Data Mining*.

Chih-Chung Chang and Chih-Jen Lin. 2011. LIBSVM: A Library for Support Vector Machines. *ACM Transactions on Intelligent Systems and Technology*. 2(3):1-27

Armand Joulin, Edouard Grave, Piotr Bojanowski, Matthijs Douze, Herve Jegou and Tomas Mikolov. 2016. FastText.zip: Compressing Text Classification Models. *arXiv preprint arXiv:1612.03651*

Svetlana Kiritchenko and Matwin Stan. 2005. Functional Annotation of Genes using Hierarchical Text Categorization. In *Proceedings of the ACL workshop on linking biological literature, ontologies and databases: Mining Biological Semantics*.

Svetlana Kiritchenko and Matwin Stan. 2006. Learning and Evaluation in the Presence of Class Hierarchies: Application to Text Categorization. In *Proceedings of the 19th Canadian conference on Artificial Intelligence, lecture Notes in Artificial Intelligence*. 4013:542-545

Leah S. Larkey and Bruce W. Croft. 1996. Combining Classifiers in Text Categorization. In *Proceedings of the 19th annual international ACM SIGIR Conference*.

Babbar Rohit, Partalas Ioannis, Gaussier Eric and Amini Massih-Reza. 2013. On Flat Versus Hierarchical Classification in Large-scale Taxonomies. In *Advances in Neural Information Processing Systems*:1824-1832.

Jurgen Schmidhuber. 2015. Deep Learning in Neural Networks. *Journal Neural Networks*. 61(C):85-117

Carlos N. Silla and Alex A. Freitas. 2011. A Survey of Hierarchical Classification Across Different Application Domains. *Data Mining and Knowledge Discovery* 22(1): 31-72.

Ioannis Tsochantaridis, Thorsten Joachinms, Thomas Hofmann, Yasemin Altun. 2005. Large Margin Methods for Structured and Interdependent Output Variables. *Journal of Machine Learning Research*. 6(2005):1453-1484

LeCun Yann, Bottou Leon, YoshuaB engio and Haffner Patrick. 1998. Gradient-based Learning Applied to Document Recognition. In *Proceedings of the IEEE*. 86(11):2278-2324

Yonghui Wu, Schuster Mike, Zhifeng Chen, Quoc V. Le and Mohammad Norouzi. 2016. Google's Neural Machine Translation System: Bridging the Gap between Human and Machine Translation. *arXiv preprint* arXiv:1609.08144.

Yoon Kim. 2014. Convolutional Neurual Networks for Sentence Classification. In *Proceedings of the 2014 Conference on Empirical Methods on Natural Language Processing*.

Zhenzhou Wu and Sean Saito. 2017. HiNet: Hierarchical Classification with Neural Network. In *the workshop of the International Conference on Learning Representations*.

SimsterQ: A Similarity based Clustering Approach to Opinion Question Answering

Aishwarya Ashok [*]
Dept of Comp Science & Engg
University of Texas at Arlington
Arlington, TX, USA
aishwarya.ashok@mavs.uta.edu

Ganapathy S. Natarajan [*]
Dept of MEIE
University of Wisconsin - Platteville
Platteville, WI, USA
natarajang@uwplatt.edu

Ramez Elmasri
Dept of Comp Science & Engg
University of Texas at Arlington
Arlington, TX, USA
elmasri@cse.uta.edu

Laurel Smith-Stvan
Dept of Linguistics and TESOL
University of Texas at Arlington
Arlington, TX, USA
stvan@uta.edu

Abstract

In recent years, there has been an increase in online shopping resulting in an increased number of online reviews. Customers cannot delve into the huge amount of data when they are looking for specific aspects of a product. Some of these aspects can be extracted from the product reviews. In this paper we introduced SimsterQ - a clustering based system for answering questions that makes use of word vectors. Clustering was performed using cosine similarity scores between sentence vectors of reviews and questions. Two variants (Sim and Median) with and without stopwords were evaluated against traditional methods that use term frequency. We also used an n-gram approach to study the effect of noise. We used the reviews in the Amazon Reviews dataset to pick the answers. Evaluation was performed both at the individual sentence level using the top sentence from Okapi BM25 as the gold standard and at the whole answer level using review snippets as the gold standard. At the sentence level our system performed slightly better than a more complicated deep learning method. Our system returned answers similar to the review snippets from the Amazon QA Dataset as measured by the cosine similarity. Analysis was also performed on the quality of the clusters generated by our system.

1 Introduction

In the recent years, the volume of online shopping has increased rapidly. This has resulted in the increase in availability of online reviews and question-answers related to a product.Traditional Question Answering (QA) systems are factual in nature. For example, "Which year did World War I end?" 1918. In opinion QA, answers to questions are based on the customers' opinions. The customers' opinions help other users to decide whether to purchase a product. This process is time consuming for the users to look at thousands of reviews to find the required information. Our paper aims at answering questions, users have, using customer reviews. We used the product reviews to extract the relevant sentences, with minimal to no overlap in meaning, and present it to the user. We make use of the AmazonQA dataset to answer binary (yes/no) questions.

The main focused contribution of this paper are:

1. Using an unsupervised clustering based system (SimsterQ) with five different variants to answer binary questions using information in the product reviews. To the best of our knowledge, we do not know of other systems that have used clustering to answer opinion based questions using product reviews.

2. Provide evidence of an unsupervised simple system having a performance akin or exceeding deep learning systems.

2 Related Work

Early work in opinion question answering addressed separating facts from opinions (Yu and Hatzivassiloglou, 2003), and the authors used a Naïve Bayes classifier to identify polarity of the opinions. Kim and Hovy (2005) aimed at identifying the opinion holder of the opinions.

Stoyanov et al. (2005) explained the differences between fact based and opinionated answers and how traditional QA systems will not be able to handle multiple perspectives for answers. Some works aimed at using community based question-answers

---

[*] These authors contributed equally to this project and paper.

Proceedings of the 3rd Workshop on e-Commerce and NLP (ECNLP 3), pages 69–76
Online, July 10, 2020. ©2020 Association for Computational Linguistics

to provide unique answers to questions (Liu et al., 2007; Somasundaran et al., 2007). Moghaddam and Ester (2011) made use of online reviews to answer questions on aspects of a product. Li et al. (2009) and Yu et al. (2012) used graphs and trees to answer opinion questions. Wan and McAuley (2016) modeled ambiguity and subjectivity in opinion QA using statistical models.

Gupta et al. (2019) give baselines for answer generation systems given the question and reviews. We use their results as the baseline for our evaluation. We also discuss the dataset from this paper in 4.2. While most systems used in the works described above are supervised learning models, our system used unsupervised learning to answer binary (yes/no) questions.

3 System Description

The answer selection process to get the top k sentences has the following steps:

1. *Relevant reviews selection:* We group all reviews by the asin/product id. We pick those reviews with the same product id as the questions.

2. *Sentence level similarity:* We process the reviews by removing punctuation and html tags. We split the reviews by sentences and find the cosine similarity between each sentence and the question.

3. *Filtering sentences below threshold:* We filter the above set by removing sentences below a threshold. The threshold is set to 0.5 so that sentences that have minimal to no similarity with the question are removed from consideration as candidate sentences.

4. *Grouping sentences with similar meaning/information:* We order the sentences by the similarity score in descending order. We then form clusters by picking the top sentence and grouping it with sentences that have high similarity (threshold value = 0.9). We repeat this until all sentences are clustered. Note that some clusters will have only one sentence at this point and some clusters may just be empty. In essence, the algorithm self selects the appropriate number of clusters.

5. *Selecting top k-sentences:* We then pick our top k = 10 answers from our top 10 clusters.

These 10 clusters in essence have the highest similarity scored sentences with the question. We either pick the first sentence in each cluster or we pick the sentence with median length from each cluster.

Our system is not limited to separate n observations into k clusters, like the k-means algorithm. N observations are naturally partitioned into up to k clusters. The algorithm naturally selects the appropriate number of clusters by grouping highly similar sentences into each cluster. We present only the sentences from the top 10 clusters; the k may be varied depending on the task at hand. In this research k was selected to be 10, so that we can compare our results with Gupta et al. (2019).

The order of the sentences in the review does not matter. We find the cosine similarity between each sentence and the question and order it from highest to lowest cosine similarity. So, the order in which the sentences occur in the review does not affect the results from our system. We use cosine similarity as it is a commonly used measure to find closeness of sentences using their angles in a vector space.

For the cosine similarity calculation,we use word2vec to calculate the sentence vector as sum of the word vectors of the words in the sentence. The calculation of sentence vector was to take advantage of the compositionality property using word2vec (Mikolov et al., 2013). We used word vectors of dimension 100 trained on the 2015 wikidump.

4 Experimental Setup

4.1 Methods Used

In our paper given a question about a product, we collected all the reviews available for that product. We then split the reviews into sentences(we will refer to these as candidate sentences) and performed five different methods of selecting candidate sentences.

Similarity (sim) made use of cosine similarity between the question and candidate sentences. The other methods were variants of this method. Similarity no stopwords (sim_ns) used the similarity method but without stopwords. Similarity median (sim_med) made use of the sentence with median length in a cluster versus the first sentence in the cluster as in sim. Similarity Median no stopwords (sim_med_ns) used the similarity median but without stopwords.

Function *Similarity (question,reviews)*:
    sentences ← split(reviews)
    sentences ← list(ordered by cosine sim)
    return sentences, cosine sim

Function *Cluster (sentences, cosine sim, threshold, median)*:
    answers ← empty
    c = 0
    while *sentences not empty* **do**
        c+=1
        cluster[c].append(sentences[0])
        for $i \leftarrow 1$ **to** *num(sentences)* **do**
            if *sim (sentences[0],sentences[i]) >* *threshold* **then**
                cluster[c].append(sentences[i])
        end
    end
    if *median == False* **then**
        answers.add(cluster[c][0])
            // Sim Variant
    else
        answers.add(cluster[c].median)
            // Median Variant
    end
    Remove sentences added to cluster c from sentences
  end
  return answers

Algorithm 1: SimsterQ Algorithm

The last method was the 3-gram method (3g). In this we split the question into 3-grams and we used the same method as sim. We used 3-gram since the shortest question in the dataset is three words long. From the clusters, we picked only sentences that have been returned by at least half the n-gram phrases. The 3-gram model was done with the idea that splitting longer questions into smaller parts will help grasp the meaning, i.e. we expected shorter phrases to incorporate more information than the whole sentence. Sim, sim_ns, sim_med, sim_med_ns, and 3g all use the SimsterQ system described in Algorithm 1. In all methods we returned the top k, where k = 10 or the maximum number of sentences available, whichever is smaller.

4.2 Dataset

The AmazonQA dataset was used in this study (Gupta et al., 2019). The dataset has both yes/no (binary) and open-ended questions. The fields we used are question id, question Type, question Text, answers, review_snippets, asin/ product id, and category. The dataset was built based on previous parallel datasets provided by Wan and McAuley (2016).

The first dataset consists of question on Amazon for products and the answers provided by users who bought those products. The second dataset was the Amazon Reviews Dataset. Amazon Reviews dataset contains 142.8 million reviews for different products in 24 product categories.

The problem with using the parallel datasets was that the evaluation was a difficult task. The answer generation by our model was using the product reviews but the gold standard is from answers written by Amazon users. For the same reason we do not use the answers as the gold standard.

The AmazonQA bridges this gap by providing relevant review snippets for each question. In addition, the dataset has a variable to identify if the question can be answered satisfactorily using the reviews alone. We found this more appropriate for our task since our intention is to provide top k sentences from the reviews that will answer a question.

We used five categories of products in our research. The five categories were Automotive, Baby, Beauty, Pet Supplies, and Tools and Home Improvement. We chose these categories as they are likely to have products that are not similar and likely to have questions that do not overlap.

We randomly picked 200 questions from each category for a total of 1000 questions. We took the reviews from the Amazon Reviews dataset since we already worked on this dataset for our previous research. The reviews were used to provide answers using the different variants of the SimsterQ system.

5 Evaluation

Evaluations were performed at both the sentence level and at the whole answer level.

5.1 Cluster Quality

Our algorithm performs clustering of sentences to find the answers. As previously mentioned, the algorithm self selects the appropriate number of clusters. However, we need to measure the quality and the number of clusters returned. Two commonly used measures to evaluate cluster quality are Silhouette score and Calinski-Harabasz score. These metrics were calculated for each question separately.

Each answer cluster was decided based on the cosine similarity with the question and the cosine similarity with the top sentence within each cluster. So, in calculating the cluster quality metrics, cosine similarity with question and cosine similarity with first sentence in the cluster were used as the features and the cluster number was used as the labels.

Silhouette score works based on distances and Calinski-Harabasz score works based on dispersion measured as squared distances (sum of squares). So we are reporting both the scores in our analysis.

5.1.1 Silhouette Score

Silhouette score measures cohesion over dispersion of each data point and provides an average measure as a normalized score between -1 and +1. Cohesion is a measure of intra-cluster distance and dispersion is a measure of inter-cluster distance. Values closer to +1 mean separated well defined clusters and values closer to -1 mean highly overlapping clusters - defeating the general purpose of clustering. If 'a' is the mean distance between a point and every other point in the same cluster, and if 'b' is the mean distance between a point and every other point in the nearest cluster, then the silhouette score for that point is defined as:

$$s = \frac{b - a}{max(a, b)} \tag{1}$$

The average s for all points is the Silhouette score for the clustering output.

5.1.2 Calinski - Harabasz Score

Calinski-Harabasz (CH) score is also called the Variance Ratio Criterion. This index provides a score calculated based on the co-variance. CH score is calculated as:

$$CH = \frac{tr(B_k)}{tr(W_k)} \frac{n - k}{k - 1} \tag{2}$$

where, B_k - co-variance matrix between clusters, W_k - co-variance matrix within clusters, n - sample size, k - number of clusters, and tr - trace of the matrix.

A higher CH score is better. The lowest possible CH score is 0 which indicates no dispersion among the clusters.

5.2 Sentence Level Evaluation

At the sentence level, we pick the top 1 sentence, using Okapi BM25, as the gold standard. To retrieve the top 1 sentence using Okapi BM25, we used the question as the query and the product reviews as the documents. Okapi BM25 is still widely used as a benchmark in similar tasks (Fan et al., 2019). An advantage of using the Okapi BM25 is that it provides us with a tf-idf based benchmark (Sixto et al., 2016). Word vectors aim to reduce problem complexity by moving away from tf-idf methods which requires us to one-hot-encode the entire vocabulary.

For each sentence in the answers returned by our system, we use the top sentence as the gold standard to calculate ROUGE-1 and ROUGE-L scores. This may seem biased, but in the absence of a gold standard we chose the proven and widely used Okapi BM25.

The average of the ROUGE scores with the max ROUGE-L F-score for each instance is reported. In addition to providing the F1 scores, Precision and Recall scores are also reported. In QA tasks, the relevance of the answers may be more important than how well the answers capture the essence of the question (a common benchmark for question answering and summarization tasks). So, P and R scores are reported to better interpret the results.

ROUGE is usually used to evaluate summarization task and may not be the best metric to measure our system performance which does a opinion based QA task which are different from the traditional QA systems. So cosine similarity was used as a metric to evaluate our system generated answer sentences against the gold standard. Three different metrics were calculated based on how well our system was able to exceed a cosine similarity threshold of 0.7 when compared against the gold standard.

To establish the cosine similarity threshold value 0.7, we used 75 questions from the Musical Instruments category (used only for bench marking purposes) and used top 5 answers that our model returns for each question. We then calculated cosine similarity between the sentences our model returned and the answer provided in the Amazon QA dataset. We took the 75th percentile value, which was 0.7, as the threshold.

5.2.1 Accuracy

Accuracy was calculated based on the total number of all answer sentences. In our case, accuracy for each method was the fraction of the sentences that had a cosine similarity, with the gold standard, of more than 0.7.

5.2.2 Correct Answer

Correct Answer was found as the fraction of questions for which our methods returned at least one answer that had a cosine similarity, with the gold standard, of more than 0.7 . This was a measure of how reliable the methods were in returning at least one relevant answer based on the reviews.

5.2.3 At least 50%

At least 50% correct answers for each question was the third evaluation metric. This was calculated as the fraction of questions for which our methods returned more than 50% of answer sentences that had a cosine similarity, with the gold standard, of more than 0.7.

The correct answer and at least 50% were inspired by the accuracy @ x% approach used by different authors working with the Amazon dataset and performing similar tasks (Fan et al., 2019; McAuley and Yang, 2016; Yu and Lam, 2018). In accuracy @ x% the commonly used measure is accuracy @ 50%. This approach helps in identifying the top answers crossing a threshold and has better relationship in real world applications (Fan et al., 2019).

5.3 Answer Level Evaluation

At the answer level, we use the review snippets returned by the AmazonQA authors as the gold standard. We calculate the ROUGE scores and cosine similarity between the gold standard and each of the five methods.

6 Results

6.1 Cluster Quality

Cluster quality was measured using the Silhouette score and the Calinski-Harabasz (CH) score. For each question, both these scores were calculated. Silhouette score cannot be calculated when there are less than two clusters. This situation arises for questions where the number of review sentences are limited. These occurrences were removed for analyzing cluster quality. All results presented on cluster quality uses a n = 647.

Figure 1a and Figure 1b show the Silhouette score and CH score for every single question. The algorithm naturally selects between 2 and 6 clusters for most of the questions and both the scores

are high in this range. Benchmarks for Silhouette scores vary by task and the hockey-stick or elbow curve is looked at to make decisions about optimal cluster sizes.

Figure 1c and Figure 1d show the mean scores plotted as a function of the number of clusters. Our algorithm naturally limits the clusters to the optimal in most cases. The optimal number of clusters is between 2 and 6, with the CH score indicating 10 clusters having a better mean. Figure 2 shows that of the 647 questions 80% of the questions have the appropriate number of clusters. Using the Pareto (80-20) rule, our algorithm's clustering quality is good, as it chooses the appropriate number of clusters 80% of the time.

6.2 Sentence Level

The sentence level evaluation was performed using the Okapi BM25 top sentence as the gold standard. Of the methods based on our system, the sim method consistently performs better than the other methods, as shown in Table 1. Except for the Correct Answer metric, sim method has the highest values in all other cases.

Our system outperforms the R-Net baseline (Rouge-L: 40.22) used by Gupta et al. (2019). Our system is supposed to be applied at the sentence level and the results indicate that a unsupervised system such as ours could outperform more complicated deep learning models. If there is a trade-off sought between computing time and accuracy, our system performs similar to or better than the baseline used by Gupta et al. (2019)

ROUGE score is not the best metric for tasks such as opinion question answering. We believe the cosine similarity is a better metric to measure how close the retrieved answer is to the gold standard. Overall the sim method is able to provide an answer more than 70% similar to the gold standard answer 91.5% of the time. From the sentences returned by our system as candidate answers, 72% of the time at least half the candidate sentences are good answers. This shows that our system is consistent and accurate at providing good answers.

6.3 Answer Level

At the answer level the top candidate sentences (up to 10) returned by our system were compared against the review snippets as the gold standard. The review snippets were top review sentences returned by the system used by Gupta et al. (2019)

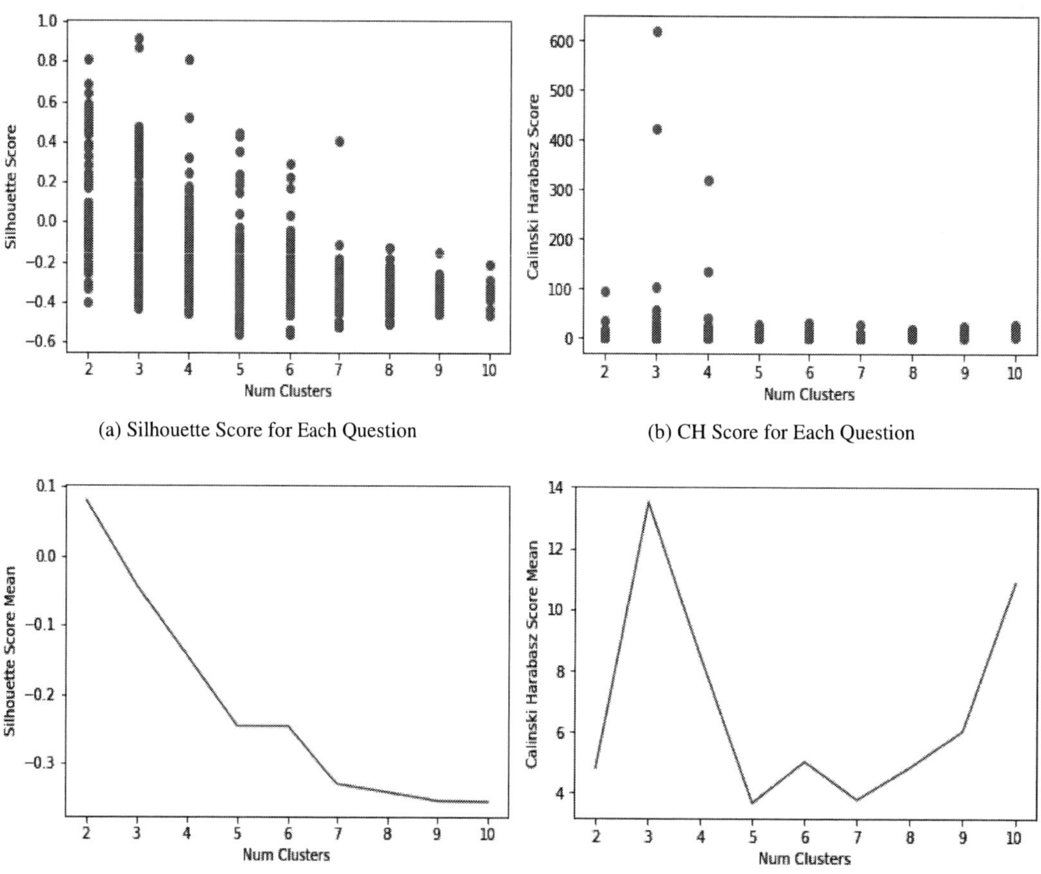

(a) Silhouette Score for Each Question   (b) CH Score for Each Question

(c) Mean Silhouette Score for Different Number of Clusters   (d) Mean CH Score for Different Number of Clusters

Figure 1: Clustering Quality Results

Table 1: Sentence Level Results

Score	Metric	Methods				
		sim	sim_ns	sim_med	sim_med_ns	3g
ROUGE-1	F	**45.86**	42.41	42.64	38.98	37.23
	P	45.94	43.17	43.04	39.88	38.72
	R	49.97	45.43	46.01	42.45	39.51
ROUGE-L	F	**42.26**	38.66	38.85	35.21	33.56
	P	44.46	41.63	41.22	38.18	36.90
	R	48.36	43.91	43.96	40.63	37.65
R-Net* ROUGE-L	F	40.22				
Similarity	Accuracy	**91.50**	82.60	91.30	82.80	87.10
	Correct Answer	83.60	72.40	**83.70**	72.90	75.50
	At least 50%	**79.77**	72.05	79.47	79.24	72.66

*This score is based on the work by (Gupta et al., 2019)

Average ROUGE scores are reported in Table 2. Both systems aim at providing the best candidate sentences. Looking at the precision scores, it is clear that our system performance is good in terms of returning relevant sentences, similar in content to the gold standard. The sim method still is the best performing method. We say this because, ROUGE-L looks for the longest common sub se-

Table 2: Answer Level Results

Score	Metric	Methods				
		sim	sim_ns	sim_med	sim_med_ns	3g
	F	38.58	34.31	**38.63**	34.24	34.89
ROUGE-1	P	63.00	65.99	62.33	65.04	61.96
	R	28.46	24.20	28.58	24.26	25.20
	F	**29.66**	25.15	29.78	25.16	26.09
ROUGE-L	P	59.72	63.28	58.99	62.18	58.74
	R	27.00	23.09	27.08	23.07	23.89
Similarity	Accuracy	**95.94**	91.02	96.36	91.19	93.88

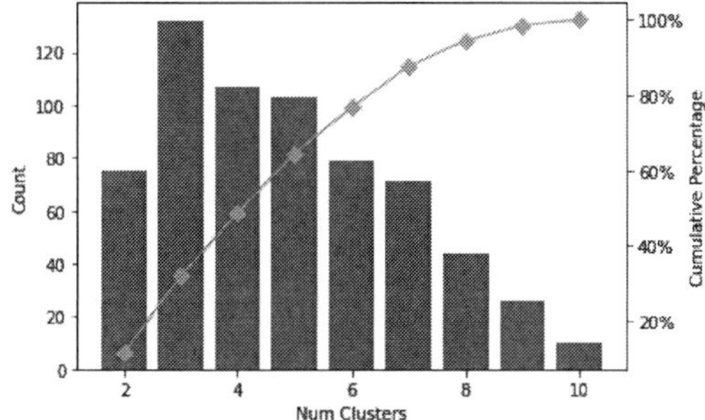

Figure 2: Pareto Chart for Number of Clusters

quence and penalizes shorter sentences. The sim method performs better with thh ROUGE-L and the accuracy metrics. Sim_med is better only with respect to the ROUGE-1 score.

Looking at the similarity scores, it is clear that the candidate sentences returned by our system is almost exactly similar to the sentences returned by Gupta et al. (2019). Once again our system is able to perform on par with a more complicated system.

7   Conclusions and Future Work

This paper introduced SimsterQ - a unsupervised clustering based system to answer questions about products by accessing the reviews of the products. Five different variants of this system were evaluated using 1000 yes/no questions. At the sentence level sim performed better with the highest ROUGE and Similarity scores. Sim method returns the top sentence from each of the 10 clusters created.

When evaluating the entire answer, our system performed better than the baseline ROUGE score from the R-Net method.

In future SimsterQ will be used with open-ended questions. The challenge with open-ended questions will be the evaluation. Perspectives expressed in the reviews need not necessarily match the perspectives in the gold standard answer. We want to evaluate the performance of SimsterQ on other datasets.

In the Amazon question/answer data set not every question has a good relevant answer. The answers are sometimes a single user's opinion. SimsterQ will be used to provide a new gold standard answer to the binary questions.

References

Miao Fan, Chao Feng, Mingming Sun, Ping Li, and Haifeng Wang. 2019. Reading customer reviews to answer product-related questions. In *Proceedings of the 2019 SIAM International Conference on Data Mining*, pages 567–575. SIAM.

Mansi Gupta, Nitish Kulkarni, Raghuveer Chanda, Anirudha Rayasam, and Zachary C. Lipton. 2019. Amazonqa: A review-based question answering task. *Proceedings of the Twenty-Eighth International Joint Conference on Artificial Intelligence*.

Soo-Min Kim and Eduard Hovy. 2005. Identifying opinion holders for question answering in opinion texts. In *Proceedings of AAAI-05 Workshop on Question Answering in Restricted Domains*, pages 1367–1373.

Fangtao Li, Yang Tang, Minlie Huang, and Xiaoyan Zhu. 2009. Answering opinion questions with random walks on graphs. In *Proceedings of the Joint Conference of the 47th Annual Meeting of the ACL and the 4th International Joint Conference on Natural Language Processing of the AFNLP: Volume 2-Volume 2*, pages 737–745. Association for Computational Linguistics.

Jingjing Liu, Yunbo Cao, Chin-Yew Lin, Yalou Huang, and Ming Zhou. 2007. Low-quality product review detection in opinion summarization. In *Proceedings of the 2007 Joint Conference on Empirical Methods in Natural Language Processing and Computational Natural Language Learning (EMNLP-CoNLL)*.

Julian McAuley and Alex Yang. 2016. Addressing complex and subjective product-related queries with customer reviews. In *Proceedings of the 25th International Conference on World Wide Web*, pages 625–635.

Tomas Mikolov, Kai Chen, Greg Corrado, and Jeffrey Dean. 2013. Efficient estimation of word representations in vector space. *arXiv preprint arXiv:1301.3781*.

Samaneh Moghaddam and Martin Ester. 2011. Aqa: aspect-based opinion question answering. In *2011 IEEE 11th International Conference on Data Mining Workshops*, pages 89–96. IEEE.

Juan Sixto, Aitor Almeida, and Diego López-de Ipiña. 2016. Improving the sentiment analysis process of spanish tweets with bm25. In *International Conference on Applications of Natural Language to Information Systems*, pages 285–291. Springer.

Swapna Somasundaran, Theresa Wilson, Janyce Wiebe, and Veselin Stoyanov. 2007. Qa with attitude: Exploiting opinion type analysis for improving question answering in on-line discussions and the news. In *ICWSM*.

Veselin Stoyanov, Claire Cardie, and Janyce Wiebe. 2005. Multi-perspective question answering using the opqa corpus. In *Proceedings of the conference on Human Language Technology and Empirical Methods in Natural Language Processing*, pages 923–930. Association for Computational Linguistics.

Mengting Wan and Julian McAuley. 2016. Modeling ambiguity, subjectivity, and diverging viewpoints in opinion question answering systems. In *2016 IEEE 16th International Conference on Data Mining (ICDM)*, pages 489–498. IEEE.

Hong Yu and Vasileios Hatzivassiloglou. 2003. Towards answering opinion questions: Separating facts from opinions and identifying the polarity of opinion sentences. In *Proceedings of the 2003 conference on Empirical methods in natural language processing*, pages 129–136. Association for Computational Linguistics.

Jianxing Yu, Zheng-Jun Zha, and Tat-Seng Chua. 2012. Answering opinion questions on products by exploiting hierarchical organization of consumer reviews. In *Proceedings of the 2012 joint conference on empirical methods in natural language processing and computational natural language learning*, pages 391–401. Association for Computational Linguistics.

Qian Yu and Wai Lam. 2018. Aware answer prediction for product-related questions incorporating aspects. In *Proceedings of the Eleventh ACM International Conference on Web Search and Data Mining*, pages 691–699.

e-Commerce and Sentiment Analysis: Predicting Outcomes of Class Action Lawsuits

Stacey Taylor
Dalhousie University
Halifax, Nova Scotia
stacey.taylor@dal.ca

Vlado Keselj
Dalhousie University
Halifax, Nova Scotia
vlado@cs.dal.ca

Abstract

In recent years, the focus of e-Commerce research has been on better understanding the relationship between the internet marketplace, customers, and goods and services. This has been done by examining information that can be gleaned from consumer information, recommender systems, click rates, or the way purchasers go about making buying decisions, for example. This paper takes a very different approach and examines the companies themselves. In the past ten years, e-Commerce giants such as Amazon, Skymall, Wayfair, and Groupon have been embroiled in class action security lawsuits promulgated under Rule 10b(5), which, in short, is one of the Securities and Exchange Commission's main rules surrounding fraud. Lawsuits are extremely expensive to the company and can damage a company's brand extensively, with the shareholders left to suffer the consequences. We examined the Management Discussion and Analysis and the Market Risks for 96 companies using sentiment analysis on selected financial measures and found that we were able to predict the outcome of the lawsuits in our dataset using sentiment (tone) alone to a recall of 0.8207 using the Random Forest classifier. We believe that this is an important contribution as it has cross-domain implications and potential, and opens up new areas of research in e-Commerce, finance, and law, as the settlements from the class action lawsuits in our dataset alone are in excess of $1.6 billion dollars, in aggregate.

1 Introduction

Since 1990, over four thousand securities class action lawsuits have been filed alleging violations of Section 10b of the Securities Exchange Act of 1934. While 10b is a very broad section, its main foci are manipulative and deceptive practices in relation to securities. In their communications with stakeholders, companies often refer to financial measures that do not conform with the Generally Accepted Accounting Principles (GAAP). These non-GAAP measures (NGMs) have been shown to positively increase a document's tone, which could be overinflating the company's prospective performance. Consequently, if actual performance falls short, overly favourable wording could be part of the instigation of securities lawsuits.

To evaluate if we could use a NGMs approach to classifying securities class action lawsuits, we use the financial filings submitted to the U.S. Securities and Exchange Commission (SEC) for ninety six random lawsuits, half settled and half dismissed, over the alleged damage period, as our dataset. We propose a novel use of sentiment analysis by examining a key section of the quarterly and annual reports submitted to the SEC in two states: first, the unaltered report as filed with the SEC (X'), and second, the report without selected NGMs (X). We then calculated the change in the tone or sentiment (as we use these terms interchangeable) as $(X - X')$ for each report and used it as an input to our prediction model. We found that we are able to predict the outcome of the lawsuits for the aggregate dataset with a recall of 0.8207 using the calculated sentiment (tone) change alone using the Random Forest classifier. When the tone change is used in conjunction with other features, we find that we are able to predict the outcome with a recall of 0.9142, again using the Random Forest classifier.

Securities lawsuits are extremely expensive to companies: the settlements from our sample alone are in excess of $1.6 billion dollars, in aggregate. To our knowledge, this use of Natural Language Processing, in particular the change in Sentiment Analysis of the NGMs in financial reports and approach to potential lawsuit classification has not been done before. We believe that this is an important contribution as it has cross-domain impli-

Proceedings of the 3rd Workshop on e-Commerce and NLP (ECNLP 3), pages 77–85
Online, July 10, 2020. ©2020 Association for Computational Linguistics

cations and potential, and opens up new areas of research in e-Commerce, finance, and law.

2 Related Work

The recurring theme of research that supports the use of NGMs is altruism — that they provide additional, relevant information that GAAP cannot (Black et al., 2018; Boyer et al., 2016; Bhattacharya et al., 2003; Frankel et al., 2004). These measures are everywhere in the financial ecosphere and have become accepted as part of the fundamental financial narrative. While the use of NGM has its supporters, there are many more detractors who cite evidence that strongly suggests that the motives are opportunistic rather than altruistic. Earnings targets are a fundamental part of measuring corporate goals. Companies set these objectives to help the company grow, but also demonstrably communicate to investors that the company is worth investing in. Researchers have found that there is a higher percentage of companies that are meeting or beating their earnings targets relative to those that do not. This strongly suggests that there is some degree of financial "management" (Burgstahler and Dichev, 1997; Brown and Caylor, 2005; Graham et al., 2005; Roychowdhury, 2006; Lougee and Marquardt, 2004; Bhattacharya et al., 2003; Davis and Tama-Sweet, 2012; Doyle et al., 2013; Black et al., 2018), and one of the tools available to do that are NGMs.

Research has also found NGMs, even as supplementary measures, are misleading given their persuasive nature (Fisher, 2016; Asay et al., 2018) as the company is essentially implying, through the adjustments that they make, that its actual performance is different (and in some cases starkly different) from its audited performance. Alee *et al.* also raises the concern that non-GAAP earnings, in particular, may confuse and mislead the average investor (Allee et al., 2007) when non-GAAP profits are created through adjustments from what was originally a GAAP loss (Young, 2014). Kang *et al.* found that when management discloses information to stakeholders, it tends to use "flexibility" in the tone in order to limit the damage by framing the negativity in positive ways (Kang et al., 2018; Li, 2016), which speaks to corporate motivation. Loughran-McDonald (2011) found that this motive entices writers to re-frame negativity into positivity because the impact of negative words on shareholders (or potential shareholders) is inexorable (Loughran and McDonald, 2011a). Therefore, careful use of word constructs can help to avoid, or at least, significantly limit the pervasive affect brought on by negative wording. This idea is also echoed by Rogers *et al.* (2011) who indicate that overly optimistic tones can be catalysts for Securities Class Action Lawsuits (Rogers and Van Buskirk, 2009).

Wongchaisuwat, Klabjan, and McGinnis used clustering classification models to determine the likelihood of patent litigation. If litigation was determined to be likely, SEC financial data was then incorporated into the model to predict the timeline to litigation (Wongchaisuwat et al., 2017). Gruginskie and Vaccaro also researched lawsuit lead time based on data provided by the Tribunal Regional Federal da 4ª Regiã from 2016 (Gruginskie and Vaccaro, 2018). Their model was broken down into four time frames: *Up to 1 Year; From 1 to 3 Years; From 3 to 5 years; and More than 5 Years.* Overall, Support Vector Machines and Random Forest returned the best F1 measure performance of 83.85 and 83.33, respectively, for results *Up to 1 Year.*

Alexander *et al.* examined features extracted from source documents such as the lawsuit itself, the trial docket, summary judgments, and the magistrate's report to predict the outcomes of a series of lawsuits (Alexander et al., 2018). Using a random forest model, they varied the number of features used in prediction to see which model would provide the most insight. The model that used the full range of features provided the best performance, resulting in 94% accuracy (Alexander et al., 2018).

3 Research Design

3.1 Methodology

Rogers, Van Buskirk, and Zechman used plantiff complaints to determine which corporate disclosures were most likely to put a firm at risk of litigation (Rogers et al., 2011). Although Rogers *et al.* did not not disclose which companies were included in their dataset, we based the main idea of our methodology on their work and used lawsuit information and corporate disclosures in conjunction with well-known dictionaries to create our dataset.

We randomly selected 96 lawsuits from the heat map on Stanford's Securities Class Action Clearinghouse (SCAC). 16 lawsuits were gathered from each of the *Top 3* sectors (Technology, Service, and Financial) and 16 lawsuits from each of the *Bottom 3* sectors (Utilities, Transportation, and Conglomerates) during the period beginning in 1990 to 2017. The following criteria were used for a company's inclusion in the dataset:

- the company had to be a public company in order for us to be able to access the company's 10-K and 10-Q reports from the SEC;

- the lawsuits had to be drawn from the *Top 3* and the *Bottom 3* sectors in the SCAC heat map;

- the class action lawsuit had to be promulgated under Rule 10b; and

- the lawsuit's status had to be either "settled" or "dismissed".

Note: *Rule 10b, which is most often addressed under Section 5, addresses deception and making false statements, among other things.* (Congress, 1951).

We then reviewed the information on the information on the SCAC to determine the *alleged* damage period and the length of the lawsuit. Both of these characteristics were then added to the dataset. The 10-K and 10-Q reports were gathered for each company that corresponded to the *alleged* damage period. Our focus was solely on the Management Discussion & Analysis (MD&A) and the Market Risks (following the research of (Loughran and McDonald, 2011a), so we parsed those sections out of the 10-K and 10-Q reports.

We curated a list of NGMs to target by using common NGMs published by Deloitte (Deloitte, 2019) as our starting point. The SEC has very specific rules regarding NGMs. In certain cases, what is normally considered to be a non-GAAP measure is, under SEC regulations, determined to be **not** non-GAAP in certain prescribed circumstances (Securities and Commission, 2018). Any NGMs that required contextualization to determine if the measure was actually non-GAAP or *not* non-GAAP under SEC regulation were removed. The following list of NGMs are considered to be *always* non-GAAP under any circumstances:

- Revised Net Income

- Earnings Before Interest and Taxes (EBIT)

- Earnings Before Interest, Taxes, and Depreciation (EBITDA)

- Earnings Before Interest, Taxes, Depreciation, Amortization, and Rent/Restructuring (EBITDAR)

- Adjusted Earnings Per Share

- Free Cash Flow (FCF)

- Core Earnings

- Funds From Operations (FFO)

- Unbilled Revenue

- Return on Capital Employed (ROCE)

- Non-GAAP

- Reconciliation

Note: "Revised" or "Adjusted" variants of measures, such as "Adjusted EBIT" were also included, as were commonly accepted variations of naming of the NGMs such as "debt-free cash flow" and "unlevered free cash flow". Also, we added the word "reconciliation" into our short list.

Using this list, sentences in the MD&A and Market Risks that contained the NGMs were then removed. Our rationale for taking this approach is that the non-GAAP measure is the focus of the sentence, and therefore, the words in that sentence exist only for discussing that measure.

To illustrate that point, we offer the following: "Our EBITDA decreased 2% for the first quarter of fiscal 2012 compared to the first quarter of fiscal 2011, due to a slight decrease in net revenues and a slight increase in operating expenses." (Taken from TD Ameritrade's 10-Q filing made on 2012-02-08.) If we take a Bag-of-Words (BoW) approach to this sentence and only remove the NGM — in this case EBITDA — that leaves the rest of the words in the sentence. Yet, without the NGM, the sentence no longer makes sense: "Our decreased 2% for the first quarter of fiscal 2012 compared to the first quarter of fiscal 2011, due to a slight decrease in net revenues and a slight increase in operating expenses."

Therefore, using the BoW approach, the words from the second non-sensical sentence would be left in when calculating the sentiment (as only the NGM keyword *EBITDA* would be removed). In reality, *all* of the words left in the sentence exist only to discuss and contextualize the NGM and need to be removed. Using both versions of the report — one with the NGMs and one without — we conducted a sentiment analysis and calculated the change in the sentiment (tone) between the MD&A and Market Risks from the report as filed with the SEC and the report with the NGMs removed *(X - X')*.

3.2 Dictionaries used for Sentiment Analysis in R

The financial lexicon and jargon used by professionals, which subsequently appears in reports, financial statements and filings (such as the 10-K and 10-Q reports we examined for our research), can be quirky and nuanced. As noted by Loughran-McDonald (Loughran and McDonald, 2011b), there are a lot of words which, out of the financial context, elicit emotional responses that may not be warranted. The word "debt" (which is a financial liability) is a good example. When used in a *business* context, the word itself is neutral; it is expected that businesses will have debt and, until that debt has been contextualized by taking into account the rest of the facts, figures, and discussions, it is not appropriate to assign it a tonal label.

We used four dictionaries provided in R to conduct our sentiment analysis, as follows:

- *Harvard-IV:* Psychological dictionary. The implementation of this dictionary in R is strictly a binary classification. There are 1,316 positive words and 1,746 negative words. Words such as *debt, interest* and *taxes* are negative words in this dictionary, and are assigned a score of -1 (Feuerriegel and Proellochs, 2019)

- *QDAP:* Collection of dictionaries that include subsets of Harvard-IV, Hu-Liu (Hu and Liu, 2004), Dolch's 220 most common words by reading level (Dolch, 1936), census data collected by the U.S. Government, among others (Feuerriegel and Proellochs, 2019). The R implementation of this dictionary is a binary classification and 1,208 positive words and 2,952 negative words. Words such as *debt, interest,* and *taxes* are negative words in this dictionary, and are assigned a score of -1 (Feuerriegel and Proellochs, 2019).

- *Henry:* Financially oriented dictionary. This dictionary has a binary classification with 53 positive words and 44 negative words. Words such as *debt, interest,* and *taxes* are, by omission, neutral words in this dictionary, and are assigned a score of 0 (Henry, 2008).

- *Loughran-McDonald:* Financially oriented dictionary. The R implementation of this dictionary is a binary classification only, with 145 positive and 885 negative words. Words such as *debt, interest,* and *taxes* are neutral words in this dictionary, and are assigned a score of 0 (Feuerriegel and Proellochs, 2019). The authors have noted, *"Language is dynamic"* and to keep up with that dynamism, they update this dictionary on an annual basis. Since 2012, no words have been deleted from their dictionary, but 343,606 words have been added and 265 words have been reclassified (Loughran and McDonald, 2018).

3.3 Dataset Characteristics

Characteristics of our prediciton model are as follows:

1. Date (date that the company filed the report with the SEC). This date is then compared to the *alleged* damage period, to determine which SEC filings are relevant to the lawsuit.

2. Central Index Key ("CIK" which acts as the company number for the SEC). The CIK is used to ensure that the reports and information gathered are for the correct company. It also facilitates calculation of the length of the lawsuit.

3. cgi (change the tone for the General Inquirer dictionary)

4. che (change in tone for the Henry dictionary)

5. clm (change in tone for the Loughran-McDonald dictionary)

6. cqdap (the change in the tone for the QDAP dictionary)

Notes: Tone changes for each dictionary is calculated as (X - X'). Also, the number of documents included in the dataset for each company was dependent on the length of the alleged damage period.

The class being predicted was the outcome of the class action lawsuit as either settled or dismissed. Please see Table 1 for the specific composition of the dataset.

Characteristic	Number/Length/Dollar Value
Total Number of Documents	2, 170
Number of documents per Sector:	
(Top 3) Services	468
(Top 3) Financial	542
(Top 3) Technology	536
(Bottom 3) Utilities	218
(Bottom 3) Transportation	248
(Bottom 3) Conglomerates	158
Longest Damage Period	46 months
Shortest Damage Period	1 month
Largest Settlement	$410 million
Smallest Settlement	$1.5 million

Table 1: Dataset Characteristics

3.4 Experiments and Evaluation Methods

We performed two different main experiments to test our model, both using 10 fold cross-validation.

The first experiment used aggregated data (all six sectors — *Top 3* and *Bottom 3*) only and leveraged all of the dictionaries. Using Naïve Bayes (NB), Random Forest (RF), and Support Vector Machines (SVM) for our predictive models, we ran a series of tests, varying the number of features used in the class prediction to determine the predictive capacity of each algorithm. In the first run, we used all features in the dataset, as outlined above to predict the outcome. We decreased the number of features used in the second run to only the sentiment and period to predict the outcome. For the third (and final run), we used only the sentiment to predict the outcome. We were particularly interested in the results for the use of sentiment alone given that the change in the sentiment score was driven by the removal of the NGM sentences.

The second experiment used the exact same parameters, reasoning, and interest as the first, with the exception of the data used. Here, we rolled up each individual sector into its major constituent of either *Top 3* (Technology, Service, and Financial) or *Bottom 3* (Utilities, Transportation, and conglomerates).

Class action lawsuits are inherently expensive (regardless of outcome). The settlements from the class action lawsuits in our dataset alone are in excess of $1.6 billion dollars, in aggregate. As indicated in Table 1, the largest individual company settlement was $410 million dollars. Our focus has been on corporate disclosure in the MD&A and Market Risks sections of the 10-K and 10-Q reports filed with the SEC. These disclosures have been meticulously reviewed by company executives, and likely auditors and the company's legal team as well before dissemination to the public. That also means that if a company is to adjust its disclosure to help shield itself from legal action, it has to be done in the drafting and (subsequent) approval stage of the MD&A and Market Risks before release to stakeholders.

From a business point of view, if the cost of **acting** is high (such as making a considerable investment), then precision is the most appropriate measure. But, if the cost of **not acting** is high (such as taking steps to avoid an overly optimistic disclosure tone prior to release), then recall is the most appropriate. Therefore, we chose recall as the most appropriate measure to evaluate our models.

We also make a distinction here between Information Retrieval (IR) and Classification. In IR, a trade-off can be made between precision and recall in that it we can simply return all documents in order to get a high recall, but a very low precision (Manning, Christopher D. and Schütze, Hinrich, 1999). However, in our classification model, we recognize that there is a corporate cost to every action that a company takes — including writing and distributing corporate disclosures. Given this, we see no tangible value for companies and investors alike if all documents are returned in order to trade precision for recall.

3.5 Results

The full results from our experiments can be found in Table 2. The *Aggregate* data results used in Experiment 1 are presented first, followed by the major constituents of *Top 3* and *Bottom 3*. The number of features ranges from all to just sentiment alone to predict the outcome (class), as denoted in the table.

Keeping in mind that *recall* is the measure that we are focusing on, we see that Random Forest (RF) is predominantly the best algorithm for this data. The results returned using RF are quite robust, returning a recall of 0.9142 for the Aggregate using all features, and 0.9938 and 0.9407 for the *Top 3* and *Bottom 3*, respectively. When using the tone change alone, the results are robust as well, returning a recall of 0.8207 for the aggregate dataset. At each node, this algorithm is designed to choose the best among randomly chosen predictors to make its decision, and then move on, to prevent overfitting. RF also works well with both numerical and categorical data, which we have. As well, because it employs a boot-strapping method (i.e. that samples are selected and then replaced to be selected again the future), and therefore makes the random tree more robust.

We varied the number of attributes used between tests, determining how far we could strip down the features in the model until the prediction dropped off significantly. The ensemble nature of this algorithm is particularly well suited to this classification task as it uses prediction by committee to overcome the shortcomings of the individual trees.

NB performed the best of all of the algorithms when classifying the Aggregate using the Sentiment Score, the Period, and the Outcome, resulting in a recall of 0.9794. NB also outperformed RF again when classifying both the Top 3 and the Bottom 3 sectors using just the Sentiment and the Outcome. We believe that this is due to the tenet of NB, which is that all of the variables are assumed to be conditionally independent. It also works well with small datasets, which we have.

SVM performed the worst out of the algorithms. The highest recall was 0.6600, was for the *Bottom 3* Sectors using the Sentiment, Period, and Outcome, but was still far off the best performing classifiers. In our dataset, there are a number of filings where the change between the "before" and "after" was zero. This means that the company did not use any of the non-GAAP measures in our extraction list. We believe that due to the fact that this type of paired data cannot be easily separated, that SVM is not well suited to our type of data.

3.6 Why This Matters

The arrival of e-Commerce changed the global marketplace forever, giving consumers access to products and services that before they would not have necessarily had access to. e-Commerce also altered the way that businesses *do business* as information that was not readily accessible like shopping habits, tools to infer decision-making, and search history, became available, allowing businesses a keen eye into *who* their customer really is. The economy has also folded in e-Commerce so well, that it is now, more than ever, dependent on it; the global pandemic COVID-19 has made this very clear. Businesses who, before the pandemic, had shied away from, or even made the conscious decision not to engage in e-Commerce have been thrust online, forcing those businesses to pivot quickly for survival.

Investors need to be appropriately protected from adverse financial investment where possible in order for the economy to stay health and strong. e-Commerce is a mainstay in the marketplace, ranging from buying goods and services online to *investing* online. It is, therefore, important that e-Commerce companies are scrutinized, alongside traditional business, to ensure the investment is sound. Sentiment analysis is an excellent tool for such scrutiny as it affords the ability to capture and demonstrate the power of sentiment of both financial professionals and the average financial investor, while allowing research to show the dichotomy that financial language and jargon have on each group's interpretation of company health, risk, and the soundness of an investment. Our research can have an impact on the different understandings of language and how it can help consumers make decisions. It also opens up new avenues of research within the domains of e-Commerce, finance, and law.

4 Conclusion

Our research provided the novel approach of performing an extractive sentiment analysis using the tone change between financial reports containing NGMs with those that do not for prediction of the outcome of Securities Class Action lawsuits promulgated under Rule 10b(5). We conducted our

Algorithm and Features Used	Precision	Recall	F1	Accuracy
Aggregate (All Features)				
Naïve Bayes	0.6049	0.8822	0.7424	0.7973
Random Forest	0.9123	**0.9142**	0.9133	0.9210
Support Vector Machine	0.6610	0.6390	0.6100	0.6439
Aggregate (Sentiment, Period)				
Naïve Bayes	0.6597	**0.9794**	0.7884	0.8172
Random Forest	0.8100	0.8879	0.8472	0.8668
Support Vector Machines	0.6235	0.6280	0.6057	0.6090
Aggregate (Sentiment)				
Naïve Bayes	0.5581	0.7152	0.6270	0.6803
Random Forest	0.6977	**0.8207**	0.7542	0.7481
Support Vector Machines	0.2693	0.5194	0.3543	0.2734
Top 3 (All Features Used)				
Naïve Bayes	0.6409	0.8822	0.7424	0.7973
Random Forest	0.9493	**0.9938**	0.9710	0.9754
Support Vector Machines	0.6220	0.6240	0.6021	0.6137
Top 3 (Sentiment, Period)				
Naïve Bayes	0.6054	0.8761	0.7160	0.7812
Random Forest	0.8149	**0.9446**	0.8750	0.8990
Support Vector Machines	0.6235	0.6280	0.6057	0.6090
Top 3 (Sentiment)				
Naïve Bayes	0.5248	**0.9610**	0.6789	0.7445
Random Forest	0.8089	0.8468	0.8274	0.8434
Support Vector Machines	0.5492	0.5492	0.4793	0.4636
Bottom 3 (All Features)				
Naïve Bayes	0.6478	0.8067	0.7185	0.7798
Random Forest	0.8819	**0.9407**	0.9104	0.9104
Support Vector Machines	0.6884	0.6568	0.6453	0.6426
Bottom 3 (Sentiment, Period)				
Naïve Bayes	0.6149	0.8306	0.7067	0.7785
Random Forest	0.8542	**0.9111**	0.8817	0.8817
Support Vector Machines	0.6905	0.6600	0.6491	0.6555
Bottom 3 (SentimentS)				
Naïve Bayes	0.5248	**0.9610**	0.6789	0.7445
Random Forest	0.8156	0.7986	0.8070	0.7993
Support Vector Machines	0.4965	0.5119	0.4040	0.5002

Table 2: Case Study Machine Learning Results

experiments on 96 random lawsuits selected from the Stanford SCAC heat map (organized by sector) from the *Top 3* and *Bottom 3* sectors, equating to 16 lawsuits per sector. We found that using the calculated change in the sentiment *(X - X′)* alone was sufficient to predict the outcome of the securities class action lawsuits to a recall of 0.8207, and when sentiment was combined with other features, recall rose to 0.9142 - both using RF.

4.1 Future Work

Taking an extractive sentiment approach, rather than a classical BoW approach, has provided new avenues of research. In this paper, we only examined the 10-K and 10-Q reports provided to the SEC. It would be valuable to apply this methodology on different aspects of e-Commerce, such as buying decisions, based on different user-groups understanding and interpretations of keywords, and how words that characterize and contextualize affect sentiment.

We also suggest that the paradigm be shifted from focusing intently on how customer information can be used to drive bottom-line performance, to incorporating how e-Commerce companies communicate with their stakeholders to determine if there is alignment between what the company says and, ultimately, does, as evidenced in their regulatory and financial filings.

References

Charlotte Alexander, Khalifeh Al Jadda, and Mohammed Javad Feizollahi. 2018. Using Text Analytics to Predict Litigation Outcomes.

Kristian D. Allee, Nilabhra Bhattacharya, Ervin L. Black, and Theodore E. Christensen. 2007. Pro Forma Disclosure and Investor Sophistication: External Validation of Experimental Evidence Using Archival Data. *Accounting, Organizations and Society*, 32(3):201 – 222.

H. Scott Asay, Robert Libby, and Kristina Rennekamp. 2018. Firm Performance, Reporting Goals, and Language Choices in Narrative Disclosures. *Journal of Accounting and Economics*, 65(2):380 – 398.

Nilabhra Bhattacharya, Ervin L Black, Theodore E Christensen, and Chad R Larson. 2003. Assessing the Relative Informativeness and Permanence of Pro Forma Earnings and GAAP Operating Earnings. *Journal of Accounting and Economics*, 36(1):285 – 319. Conference Issue on.

Dirk E. Black, Theodore E. Christensen, Jack T. Ciesielski, and Benjamin C. Whipple. 2018. Non-GAAP Reporting: Evidence from Academia and Current Practice. *Journal of Business Finance & Accounting*, 45(3-4):259–294.

Benoit Boyer, Ralph Lim, and Lyons Bridget. 2016. A Case Study in the Use and Potential Misuse of Non-GAAP Financial Measures. *Journal of Applied Business and Economics*, 18(3):117–126.

Lawrence D. Brown and Marcus L. Caylor. 2005. A Temporal Analysis of Quarterly Earnings Thresholds: Propensities and Valuation Consequences. *The Accounting Review*, 80(2):423–440.

David Burgstahler and Ilia Dichev. 1997. Earnings Management to Avoid Earnings Decreases and Losses. *Journal of Accounting and Economics*, 24(1):99 – 126. Properties of Accounting Earnings.

United States Congress. 1951. 17 CFR § 240.10b-5 - Employment of Manipulative and Deceptive Devices.

Angela K. Davis and Isho Tama-Sweet. 2012. Managers' Use of Language Across Alternative Disclosure Outlets: Earnings Press Releases Versus MD&A. *Contemporary Accounting Research*, 29(3):804–837.

Deloitte. 2019. A Roadmap to Non-GAAP Financial Measures.

Edward W Dolch. 1936. A Basic Sight Vocabulary. *The Elementary School Journal*, 36(6):456–460.

Jeffrey T. Doyle, Jared N. Jennings, and Mark T. Soliman. 2013. Do Managers Define Non-GAAP Earnings To Meet or Beat Analyst Forecasts? *Journal of Accounting and Economics*, 56(1):40 – 56.

Stefan Feuerriegel and Nicolas Proellochs. 2019. *Package 'SentimentAnalysis*.

Alex Fisher. 2016. Non-GAAP Measures: Academic Literature Review (1996-2016).

Richard M. Frankel, Sarah McVay, and Mark T. Soliman. 2004. Street Earnings and Board Independence.

John R. Graham, Campbell R. Harvey, and Shiva Rajgopal. 2005. The Economic Implications of Corporate Financial Reporting. *Journal of Accounting and Economics*, 40(1):3 – 73.

Lúcia Adriana dos Santos Gruginskie and Guilherme Luís Roehe Vaccaro. 2018. Lawsuit Lead Time Prediction: Comparison of Data Mining Techniques Based on Categorical Response Variable. *PLOS ONE*, 13(6):1 – 26.

Elaine Henry. 2008. Are Investors Influenced By How Earnings Press Releases Are Written? *The Journal of Business Communication (1973)*, 45(4):363–407.

Minqing Hu and Bing Liu. 2004. Mining Opinion Features in Customer Reviews. In *AAAI*, volume 4, pages 755–760.

Taeyoung Kang, Do-Hyung Park, and Ingoo Han. 2018. Beyond the Numbers: The Effect of 10-K Tone on Firms' Performance Predictions Using Text Analytics. *Telematics and Informatics*, 35(2):370 – 381.

Feng Li. 2016. Do Stock Market Investors Understand the Risk Sentiment of Corporate Annual Reports?

Barbara A. Lougee and Carol A. Marquardt. 2004. Earnings Informativeness and Strategic Disclosure: An Empirical Examination of "Pro Forma" Earnings. *The Accounting Review*, 79(3):769–795.

Tim Loughran and Bill McDonald. 2011a. Barron's Red Flags: Do They Actually Work? *Journal of Behavioral Finance*, 12(2):90–97.

Tim Loughran and Bill McDonald. 2011b. When
Is a Liability Not a Liability? Textual Analysis,
Dictionaries, and 10-Ks. *The Journal of Finance*,
66(1):35–65.

Tim Loughran and Bill McDonald. 2018. Documenta-
tion for the LoughranMcDonald Master Dictionary.

Manning, Christopher D. and Schütze, Hinrich. 1999.
*Foundations of Statistical Natural Language Pro-
cessing*. The MIT Press.

Jonathan L. Rogers and Andrew Van Buskirk. 2009.
Shareholder Litigation and Changes in Disclosure
Behavior. *Journal of Accounting and Economics*,
47(1):136 – 156. Accounting Research on Issues of
Contemporary Interest.

Jonathan L. Rogers, Andrew Van Buskirk, and Sarah
L. C. Zechman. 2011. Disclosure Tone and
Shareholder Litigation. *The Accounting Review*,
86(6):2155–2183.

Sugata Roychowdhury. 2006. Earnings Management
Through Real Activities Manipulation. *Journal of
Accounting and Economics*, 42(3):335 – 370.

U.S. Securities and Exchange Commission. 2018. Non-
GAAP Financial Measures.

P. Wongchaisuwat, D. Klabjan, and J. O. McGinnis.
2017. Predicting Litigation Likelihood and Time to
Litigation for Patents. In *Proceedings of the 16th
Edition of the International Conference on Articial
Intelligence and Law*, ICAIL '17, page 257–260,
New York, NY, USA. Association for Computing
Machinery.

Steven Young. 2014. The Drivers, Consequences and
Policy Implications of Non-GAAP Earnings Reporting. *Accounting and Business Research*, 44(4):444–
465.

On Application of Bayesian Parametric and Non-parametric Methods for User Cohorting in Product Search

Shashank Gupta

Flipkart Internet Private Limited

India

shashank.gupta@flipkart.com

Abstract

In this paper, we study the applicability of Bayesian Parametric and Non-parametric methods for user clustering in an E-commerce search setting. To the best of our knowledge, this is the first work which presents a comparative study of various Bayesian clustering methods in the context of product search. Specifically, we cluster users based on their topical patterns from their respective product search queries. To evaluate the quality of the clusters formed, we perform collaborative query recommendation task. Our findings indicate that simple parametric model like Latent Dirichlet Allocation (LDA) outperforms more sophisticated non-parametric methods like Distance Dependent Chinese Restaurant Process and Dirichlet Process based clustering in both tasks.

1 Introduction

Online retail business has been on an unprecedented growth since last few years, with a market share of 600 Billion dollars last year in the United States [1]. To cope up with such an epochal growth, product discovery becomes an important aspect for any e-commerce platform. It is an important aspect to help customers navigate an ever increasing inventory of products.

Product search is an important aspect of E-Commerce discovery, where displaying relevant and personalized products in answer to an user query is directly tied to customer satisfaction (Su et al., 2018; Moe, 2003).

Personalizing search results entails mining search behavior logs to represent individual user's search intent. However, due to the large variance in individual user's preference, finding a good representation is often difficult. In the context of web

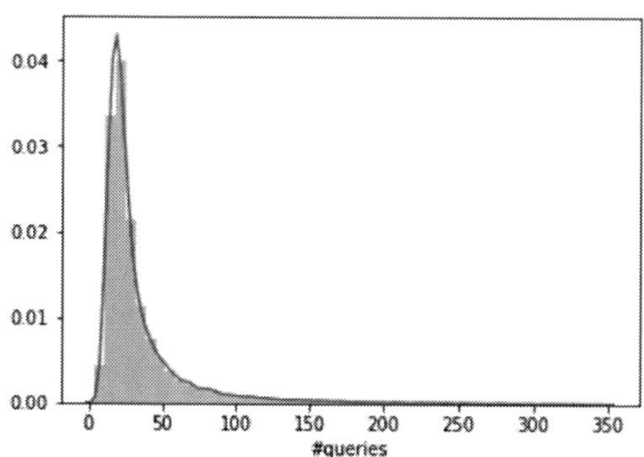

Figure 1: Query Distribution across users.

search, search intent mining has been extensively studied (Teevan et al., 2008; White and Drucker, 2007; Joachims et al., 2017).

However, despite it's apparent importance, personalization in product search is not very well studied. There has been some attempts to model user's search intent based on her past product interactions. Qingyao et al. (Ai et al., 2017) jointly learn representations of user, query and users' product reviews for personalization. In a follow-up work, Qingyao et al. (Ai et al., 2019), learn a 'zero-attention' model for representation learning to account to cold-start problem in new product categories. However, it should be noted that both work attempt to model search interest at the granularity of individual users, which are highly spare in nature.

Fig. 1 is the distribution of queries across users in the Amazon Product Search Dataset (Ai et al., 2017). The distribution is skewed towards left side of the distribution. It shows that query distribution across users is sparse, with very few users have high number of queries and subsequently few interactions as-well. This makes it challenging to model search interests at the granularity of individual users.

By modelling each user separately, we are also

[1] https://www.digitalcommerce360.com/article/us-ecommerce-sales/

Proceedings of the 3rd Workshop on e-Commerce and NLP (ECNLP 3), pages 86–89

Online, July 10, 2020. ©2020 Association for Computational Linguistics

missing on the chance to capture the heterogeneity in the user's search interests. Modelling user's jointly can aid in learning individual user's interest, as-well as aid in handling sparsity through sharing statistical strength within the group. Towards this end, we study various Bayesian clustering methods to model latent user cohorts by mining user's search query patterns.

To the best of our knowledge, this is the first work in the domain of E-Commerce search to study the application of bayesian methods for modelling user cohorts. The aim of this paper is to present a comparative study of different bayesian parametric and non-parametric methods in the domain of product search. Product search system designers can benifit from this study by making an informed decision when designing E-commerce personalization system.

2   Related Work

There has been plenty of work in web search for modelling user cohorts for learning an effective ranking function. Previous studies (Bian et al., 2010; Giannopoulos et al., 2011) propose a K-means clustering of queries and then a learn a ranking function within each sub-group to capture query patterns in each group.

However, the focal unit of the previous work is queries, whereas we are interested in modelling user. The closest to our work is by Yan et al. (Yan et al., 2014), where they model user cohorts based on Click-Through Rates (CTR) and Open Directory Project (ODP) based topics. However, instead of relying on human curated ODP based topics, we use probabilistic topic models to identify topics from user's log data and further use it for clustering.

Towards this end, in this work, we study the problem of user cohorting by clustering user's queries in the probabilistic topic space. Specifically, we study application of various probabilistic topic models like Latent Dirichlet Allocation (LDA) (Blei et al., 2003), Hierarchical Dirichlet Process (HDP) (Wang et al., 2011; Teh, 2006), Dirichlet Process Gaussian Mixture Model (DPGMM) (Teh, 2010) and the more recent Distance Dependent Chinese Restaurant Process (ddCRP) (Blei and Frazier, 2011). To the best of our knowledge, this is the first work in product search which studies application of probabilistic topic models for user cohorting.

3   User Cohorting using Probabilistic Topic Models

In this section, we will formally define the problem statement followed by a brief description of the non-parametric ddCRP user clustering method.

3.1   Problem Statement:

We define the search log D as : $D = \{u, q, p\}$, where u is the individual user identifier, q is the product search query and p is the unique id of the product purchased by the user in the context of the query q fired. As part of pre-processing, we aggregate the queries fired by user as basic representation unit. Each user u_i is represented as, $u_i = \{q_1, q2, ..., q_n\}$, where each query q_j is represented by bag-of-words of of basic search tokens. Here, the user can be treated as a document of search tokens. The goal is to cluster users' based on topical representation.

3.2   ddCRP for user clustering

In this section, we will describe the ddCRP method for user clustering.

The ddCRP is an extension of the popular Bayesian Non-parametric method Chinese Restaurant Process (CRP). Like CRP, it is defined as a distribution over all possible partitions of a set (users in our case). Customer (user u_i in our case) enter the restaurant in a sequence and select a table z_i following another customer (user) u_j based on some probability and sits on that table. This is unlike CRP, where the probability of a customer choosing a seat is proportional to number of customers already seated on that seat.

Formally, the ddCRP process can be summarized by the following mathematical notation:

$$p(z_i = j | D, \alpha) \propto \begin{cases} f(d_{ij}), & \text{if } i \neq j \\ \alpha, & otherwise \end{cases} \quad (1)$$

where z_i is the latent table assignment for the customer i. $z_i = j$ represents that the customer i is linked to customer j with probability defined above. D is the matrix of all pairwise distances (defined in the next section) and alpha is the hyper-parameter of the model. f is the decay function and d_{ij} is the pre-defined distance between user u_i and the user u_j. $R(u_{1:N})$ defines the clustering structure by traversing the final user linking generated by the model.

The generative story of the ddCRP model is defined as below:

1. For $i \in [1 : N]$, sample $z_i \sim$ ddCRP(α, f, D).

2. For $i \in [1 : N]$

   (a) Draw parameter from the base distribution, $\theta_i \sim G_0$

   (b) For each of the M words in the user query chain, draw $w_i \sim$ F(θ_i).

Here, since we are dealing with bag-of-words model of text, we choose G_0 as a dirichlet distribution and F to be a Multinomial distribution, which can generate the words in the user's query chain.

3.3 Defining the Distance Function

To fully specify the ddCRP model, we need to define the distance function. In our case, to define the distance between two users as Hellinger distance between their LDA topic distribution.

4 Experiments

In this section, we will describe the experimental results from our study.

4.1 Dataset

For experiments, we use the product search dataset described by Qingyao et. al (Ai et al., 2017). They use the Amazon product review dataset and extract queries from the user's product reviews and use the purchased product as the relevant product. The dataset is generated for multiple product categories, we choose two of them for our experiments: 1) Compact Discs (CDs) and Vinyls. 2) Kindle Dataset. We removed users with atleast 200 queries, which leaves us with 1300 users in both datasets.

We select the following two tasks to evaluate performance of the clustering method: 1) Collaborative Query Recommendation and 2) Collaborative Document Recommendation.

For each user, we select a random sample of 5% queries as test queries and 95% for training. Similarly for products. We train LDA model on query chain constructed from training queries of each user. Specifically, we treat a simple concatenation of queries in user's training queries as a document and the collective query chain of all users as the corpus.

4.2 Collaborative Query Recommendation:

Once the users are segmented into various groups, we compute frequency of queries in each group. Each user is recommended top-K queries computed from his respective group. We treat user's test query as relevant queries and compute the performance of recommended queries against the relevance set.

Method	Prec@5	Prec@10
LDA	0.071934	0.088187
HDP	0.044093	0.058691
ddCRP	0.040030	0.056057
LDA + IGMM	0.007073	0.008202
LDA + GMM	0.017156	0.020767

Table 1: Query Recommendation Performance for CDs data

Method	Prec@5	Prec@10
LDA	0.072863	0.088133
HDP	0.069046	0.079751
ddCRP	0.054440	0.063734
LDA + IGMM	0.031701	0.027718
LDA + GMM	0.009627	0.011535

Table 2: Query Recommendation Performance for the Kindle data

5 Results

We present some preliminary results on the query recommendation task on the two datasets mentioned above. We compare the following methods:

1) LDA: We use the MAP estimates from the posterior over topics for each user to get the cluster assignment.

2) HDP: Similar to LDA, we use MAP estimates from the posterior to get the cluster assignment.

3) LDA + GMM: We perform Gaussian Mixture Model (GMM) clustering with LDA topic distribution as feature vector.

4) LDA + IGMM: We use Infinite Gaussian Mixture model, which is a non-parameteric model to perform clustering over user's topic distributions.

From the results, it is clear that LDA outperforms more sophisticated Non-parameteric methods in terms of Precision metric.

6 Conclusion

This paper can serve as a starting point of discussion around the use of Bayesian Non-parametric models for user cohorting. The prelimary results weigh in favor of simple parametric model like LDA, however, we believe that with further investigation, ddCRP method's performance can be improved. More specifically, if we perform clustering in the space of recently proposed neural embedding methods, instead of conventional topic model space, it's performance can be improved. We hope this paper can start that discussion.

References

Qingyao Ai, Daniel N Hill, SVN Vishwanathan, and W Bruce Croft. 2019. A zero attention model for personalized product search. In *Proceedings of the 28th ACM International Conference on Information and Knowledge Management*, pages 379–388.

Qingyao Ai, Yongfeng Zhang, Keping Bi, Xu Chen, and W Bruce Croft. 2017. Learning a hierarchical embedding model for personalized product search. In *Proceedings of the 40th International ACM SIGIR Conference on Research and Development in Information Retrieval*, pages 645–654.

Jiang Bian, Xin Li, Fan Li, Zhaohui Zheng, and Hongyuan Zha. 2010. Ranking specialization for web search: a divide-and-conquer approach by using topical ranksvm. In *Proceedings of the 19th international conference on World wide web*, pages 131–140.

David M Blei and Peter I Frazier. 2011. Distance dependent chinese restaurant processes. *Journal of Machine Learning Research*, 12(Aug):2461–2488.

David M Blei, Andrew Y Ng, and Michael I Jordan. 2003. Latent dirichlet allocation. *Journal of machine Learning research*, 3(Jan):993–1022.

Giorgos Giannopoulos, Ulf Brefeld, Theodore Dalamagas, and Timos Sellis. 2011. Learning to rank user intent. In *Proceedings of the 20th ACM international conference on Information and knowledge management*, pages 195–200.

Thorsten Joachims, Laura Granka, Bing Pan, Helene Hembrooke, and Geri Gay. 2017. Accurately interpreting clickthrough data as implicit feedback. In *ACM SIGIR Forum*, volume 51, pages 4–11. Acm New York, NY, USA.

Wendy W Moe. 2003. Buying, searching, or browsing: Differentiating between online shoppers using in-store navigational clickstream. *Journal of consumer psychology*, 13(1-2):29–39.

Ning Su, Jiyin He, Yiqun Liu, Min Zhang, and Shaoping Ma. 2018. User intent, behaviour, and perceived satisfaction in product search. In *Proceedings of the Eleventh ACM International Conference on Web Search and Data Mining*, pages 547–555.

Jaime Teevan, Susan T Dumais, and Daniel J Liebling. 2008. To personalize or not to personalize: modeling queries with variation in user intent. In *Proceedings of the 31st annual international ACM SIGIR conference on Research and development in information retrieval*, pages 163–170.

Yee Whye Teh. 2006. A hierarchical Bayesian language model based on pitman-yor processes. In *Proceedings of the 21st International Conference on Computational Linguistics and 44th Annual Meeting of the Association for Computational Linguistics*, pages 985–992, Sydney, Australia. Association for Computational Linguistics.

Yee Whye Teh. 2010. Dirichlet process.

Chong Wang, John Paisley, and David Blei. 2011. Online variational inference for the hierarchical dirichlet process. In *Proceedings of the Fourteenth International Conference on Artificial Intelligence and Statistics*, pages 752–760.

Ryen W White and Steven M Drucker. 2007. Investigating behavioral variability in web search. In *Proceedings of the 16th international conference on World Wide Web*, pages 21–30.

Jinyun Yan, Wei Chu, and Ryen W White. 2014. Cohort modeling for enhanced personalized search. In *Proceedings of the 37th international ACM SIGIR conference on Research & development in information retrieval*, pages 505–514.

Author Index

Ahsan, Unaiza, 19
Al Jadda, Khalifeh, 19
Alt, Christoph, 1
Ashok, Aishwarya, 69

Banerjee, Jyotirmoy, 35
Beaulieu, Marie, 7

Condylis, Paul C., 59
Cui, Xiquan, 19

Elmasri, Ramez, 69

Fu, Yuyangzi, 54

Gao, Dehong, 64
Gautam, Akash, 46
Gosangi, Rakesh, 46
Goyal, Pawan, 35
Guo, Mingming, 19
Gupta, Shashank, 86

Hennig, Leonhard, 1
Hidayat, Albert, 59
Hu, Changjian, 1

Jia, Yanan, 24

Kerianto, Muhamad Danang, 59
Keselj, Vlado, 77
Kong, Sheng-yi, 59
Kumar, Surender, 35

Lee, Seong Per, 59
Leo, Marie Stephen, 59

Mahata, Debanjan, 46
Meng, Yao, 1
Munawwar, Eram, 59

Nadkarni, Prajit, 35
Natarajan, Ganapathy, 69

Pai, Nithish, 35

Ramtej, Jaidam, 35
Roy, Kalyani, 35

Shah, Rajiv Ratn, 46
Shah, Smit, 35
Sharma, Arpit, 40
Smith-Stvan, Laurel, 69
Sun, Meng, 59

Tagliabue, Jacopo, 7
Taylor, Stacey, 77

Wang, Chao, 1
Wang, Tian, 54
West, Rebecca, 19
Wu, San He, 19

Yan, Nian, 19
Yu, Bingqing, 7

Zhang, Hanchu, 1

Association for Computational Linguistics
209 N. Eighth Street
Stroudsburg, Pennsylvania 18360

ISBN 978-1-7138-1384-2